VERMONT

The State with the Storybook Past

illustrated by Robert MacLean

with a Foreword by H. N. Muller
The University of Vermont

The Stephen Greene Press
Brattleboro, Vermont

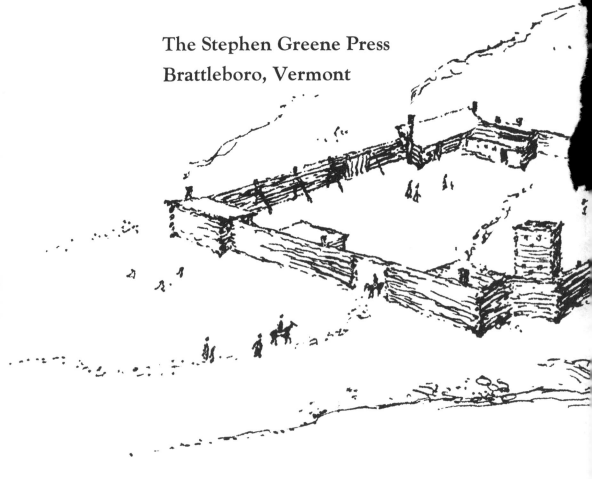

VERMONT

The State with the Storybook Past

by Cora Cheney

Dedication

To the librarians of Vermont, especially Vivian Bryan of the Vermont State Library, without whose help this book could not have been written.

PUBLISHED SEPTEMBER 1976
Second printing August 1979

This book has been produced in the United States of America: designed by Robert L. Dothard Associates, composed by American Book–Stratford Press, and printed and bound by The Murray Printing Company. It is published by The Stephen Greene Press, Brattleboro, Vermont 05301.

LIBRARY OF CONGRESS CATALOGING IN PUBLICATION DATA

Cheney, Cora.
  Vermont, the state with the storybook past.

  Bibliography: p.
  SUMMARY: Examines the history of Vermont from the days when Indians roamed the country to 1970 when Act 250, a landmark in environmental legislation, was passed.
  1. Vermont—History—Juvenile literature.
[1. Vermont—History] I. Title.
F49.3.C45   974.3   76-13804
ISBN 0-8289-0283-6

Contents

Foreword   xi

1. Indians, Frenchmen, and Englishmen   3
   The Land   3
   The Indians   6
   Champlain, the Frenchman   11
   The Mystery of Johne Graye   12
   Father Jogues   14
   French Settlements   16
   English Settlements, the Stage for War   17
   War and Captives   19
   Fort Dummer   20
   More Captives   22
   Rogers' Rangers and Indian Fighting   23
   Chief Greylock   24
   Victory for England   25

2. The New Hampshire Grants, New York, and
   Ethan Allen   27
   Benning Wentworth   27
   New York Steps In   31
   A Man Named Ethan Allen   34

The Green Mountain Boys   37
Life in the Grants   41
The Tale of Ann Story   43
The Westminster "Massacre"   44

3. Ticonderoga   50
Ethan's Idea   50
Spy Noah Phelps   51
Samuel Beach   51
Benedict Arnold   52
Nathan Beeman   53
Victory!   54
More Success—and a Failure   55

4. The New Hampshire Grants Become
Vermont   57
Seth Warner, the New Leader   57
Fighting in Canada   59
Fort Independence   61
Conventions and Government   63
The Battle of Valcour   64
The Vote for Independence at Westminster   66
Vermont Gets a Name   67
Burgoyne   69
Vermont Gets a Constitution   71

5. The Republic of Vermont   74
Ira Saves the Day   74
The Battle of Bennington   76
Vermont's First Elections and Assembly   78

Border Problems   79
The Return of Ethan Allen   81
The Haldimand Plot   83
The Story of Zadock Steele   85
Yorker Warfare   86
The End of the Revolution   88
Elias Smith   89
Stamps, Money, and New Shoes   91
Vermont, the Fourteenth State   94

6. From Statehood to the Civil War   95

Some Special People   95
   Matthew Lyon and the New Century   95
   The Story of Fanny Allen   97
   Green Mountain Inventors   98
   Zerah Colburn, Unhappy Genius   100
   Zadock Thompson, a Boy Who Liked to Collect Things   101
Special Happenings   103
   The State House   103
   Smuggling and the War of 1812   105
   The Runaway Pond   106
   The Year of No Summer   107
   Daniel Webster Comes to Call   108
   The Canadian Rebellion   110
What Vermonters Thought   110
   Churches of the Early Years   110
   Free-Thinkers and New Religions   112
   Women and Their Ideas   114
   Problems for Children and Parents   116
   Schools and Libraries   117
How Vermonters Lived   120
   Vermont Roads   120
   Taking in Boarders   121
   Marvels of the Age   123
   The Morgan Horse   126
   Merino Sheep   127
   Water Travel   128
   The Coming of the Railroads   129
   Emigration   131

7. Vermont and the Civil War   133
   Anti-Slave Vermont   133
   The Underground Railroad   134
   Vermont Goes to War   136
   Drummer Boys   139
   The Sleeping Sentinel   139
   The St. Albans Raid   141
   Hospitals for Soldiers   142
   Vermont Nurses   143
   A Romantic Story   144
   The End of the War   147

8. Who Are the People Who Made
   Vermont?   148
   What's a Vermonter?   148
   Scots   149
   Three Black Men   149
   Franco-Americans   152
   The Irish in Vermont   153
   "The Know-Nothings"   154
   The Fenian Problems   155
   Swedes and Finns   156
   Slate Brings the Welsh   156
   Granite and the Vermont Italians   157
   Marble and the Vermont "United Nations"   158
   Jews in Vermont   159
   Poles and Spaniards   159
   And New Faces Keep Coming   160

9. Life, People, and Politics after the
   Civil War   162

   A Few Luxuries   162
   Happiness, Holidays, and a Special Birthday   164
   The Grange   166
   Senator Justin Smith Morrill   167
   President Chester Arthur   168
   George Perkins Marsh, Conservationist   169
   Carrie Burnham Kilgore, Lawyer   170
   Abby Hemenway, Historian and Editor   171
   More Busy Women   172
   Annie Ide and Her Perfectly Marvelous Present   172
   Mr. Kipling in Vermont   174
   Mrs. McKinley's Butter   174
   Admiral George Dewey   175
   The End of the Century   176

10. Vermont in the 20th Century   177

    Through World War I   177
       Molly Robinson, Being a Vermont Girl   177
       Automobiles   179
       Railroads   181
       Snowflake Bentley   183
       Outdoors, Winter and Summer   186
       Young People Get Together   187
       Aviation   189
       World War I   191

From the 1920's Through the Great Depression   192
  Women Get the Vote, and More!   192
  Movies Come to Vermont   193
  Early Radio in Vermont   194
  President Calvin Coolidge   196
  The Flood of 1927   197
  The Civilian Conservation Corps and the Depression   197
  The Green Mountain Parkway   199
From World War II to Act 250   200
  The War   200
  A Poet, and Two Statesmen   201
    ROBERT FROST   201
    WARREN AUSTIN   202
    GEORGE D. AIKEN   203
  Vermont, the Beckoning Country   204
  The End, and a Beginning   206

Acknowledgments   207
Appendix I. An Explanation of Act 250   209
Appendix II. A Chronology   211
Appendix III. Some Facts About Vermont   220
Appendix IV. Some Books About Vermont   223
About the Author   225
Index   227

Vermont: The State with the Storybook Past is endorsed by the Vermont Bicentennial Commission. The research and writing of this book were funded in part by a grant from the Vermont Bicentennial Commission. Logotype © 1974 Vermont Bicentennial Commission.

Foreword

History, along with the Three R's, has traditionally been drummed into children to the strict cadence of the hickory stick. Generations of youngsters have drilled to the same old questions, which seemingly bore little direct relationship to the sights and rhythm of the playground, the meandering walk home, and the other more immediate concerns of growing up in America. When was the Spanish Armada defeated? —Who was the fifth or tenth President of the United States? —What happened at Bennington (but not really Bennington) in 1777? These questions brought correctly memorized responses from diligent young scholars and stammering shame to others. Usually history became a "subject," an exercise in names and dates to be pushed happily in a forgotten corner of the school desk for the summer, not to be retrieved until another teacher asked the same questions again.

Cora Cheney deserves our gratitude and congratulations for breaking this tragic cycle with *Vermont: The State with the Storybook Past*. Our past, our history, is far too important to become the cornerstone of educational tedium. Side by side with acquiring fundamental skills and a common information base, the best education brings an individual to self-knowledge—a sense of himself and his relationship to his surroundings. The educational experience should help each student arrive at highly individual (if tentative) answers to the elemental queries, "Where do I come from?" "Who am I?" and "Where am I going?" Answers to these questions depend on history. Each of us, individually or in groups, is the sum of our past. To understand ourselves and our society, and to make informed decisions for the present and the future, we must have a sense of the past.

Vermont: The State with the Storybook Past is an historical study of Vermont that speaks directly to young people: it is not a juvenile version of the standard (and inadequate) histories of the State. The story begins with a discussion of Act 250, Vermont's landmark legislation of 1970, which has attracted national attention. Quickly the story moves to prehistory and Indians, the frequently neglected first-known inhabitants of the area. Following a chronological path, the narrative travels to the present. Vermont's history then becomes the events that preceded Act 250 and thus are subtly tied to the present. For Cora Cheney history is not the passive, abstract, and impersonal matter which all too frequently rests between the covers of texts. Even books that manage to touch a child's expanding imagination with rich tales of kings and knights, of explorers and vanished empires, or of the Green Mountain Boys and the American Revolution too seldom translate the intrinsic fascination of the past to immediate and presumably more mundane affairs.

In this sense, however, Cora Cheney is a gifted translator. Dialogue, mostly invented for the purpose but not historically misleading, has created life-size people from famous and ordinary characters alike. Wherever the written record has provided suitable, easily read prose, she has worked it into the narrative. Ethan and Ira Allen, Senator Justin S. Morrill, and former Governor Deane C. Davis all speak as well as act. Their impact becomes immediate instead of distant, thus allowing children to identify easily with them.

At long last the neglected heroine and housewife take their positions alongside the heroes and the "common man" in the story of Vermont's past; the distorting preponderance of men in our history is happily redressed. Children, roughly half of whom are girls, can read about Ann Story, Clarina Howard Nichols, Abby Hemenway, Carrie Burnham Kilgore, Consuelo Northrop Bailey, and a host of others—including Estelle S. Johnson, Lydia A. Wood, and Amanda Colburn, who braved the gore of army hospitals to nurse Civil War soldiers. The large cast of characters also demonstrates that children played recognizable roles.

Further, purely Yankee stock and old-line New England tradition are joined and enriched by men and women of other races and backgrounds. Cora Cheney's treatment shows how the Green Mountains and long valleys of Vermont have become the home of Blacks, of Scots, Swedes, Finns, Poles, Italians, as well as Irish, French-Canadians, and Jews.

Many texts, especially those for readers in their "formative years," confuse history with a lesson in civics. History's best teaching lies in the reality of its example, not in a continuous chronicle of the great events of government and famous military actions. *Vermont: The State with the Storybook Past* deals with schools, recreation, roads, Sunday school, and other elements of everyday life. The broad range of material presents something for everyone and keeps things in a manageable, human perspective for the young reader. The book is plainly relevant to Vermont's children.

The details of Vermont's past may be unique, but as well-written history they portray the universal qualities of human nature. Children everywhere can easily identify with the robust antics of the Green Mountain Boys and their boisterous leader, Ethan Allen, or with the crucial events of the

American Revolution played out in the Champlain Valley. They can also sense the cold fear of Indian raids, the drama and hardship of migration, and the recurring seasonal tasks of Vermont farm life. But Vermont also has a greater story to tell.

In more than two hundred years the hardy inhabitants of the Green Mountains have not lost sight of certain fundamental propositions. Vermont's first settlers were attracted by the availability of good land, which, when properly tended (or even judiciously bought and sold), promised a man and his family that measure of freedom afforded by economic independence. Love of the land and desire for freedom remain strong. Even the thousands who migrate to Vermont for a short vacation or with the intention to stay are still attracted by the continuing sense of place and independence.

The realities of the eighteenth century are not those of the twentieth, and the notion of freedom has taken a more contemporary definition. Freedom from hunger and from want have joined such long-standing rights as freedom of speech and of assembly. The struggle for control of land provided the impetus for Vermont's independence in the 1770's. Two hundred years later Vermonters are still working to preserve the land from another set of threats. In the interim they declared and protected their freedom, experimenting with new concepts and adjusting to changing conditions. They were the first to remove property qualifications from the franchise, and were the first to make slavery contrary to the law of the State. Other ideas whose day had not yet come (for many it never arrived) found a platform, and even followers, in Vermont. These sober Yankees allowed a man the special freedom to make a "damn fool of himself."

Vermont: The State with the Storybook Past is an important book. The State has a story to tell, and for a long time it has needed to tell it to its youth. Perhaps even more importantly, this is a book that can help young readers to develop a sense of history, which is an essential part of understanding themselves and the world around them.

H. N. MULLER
Director, Living and Learning Center
The University of Vermont

It was an early spring morning in Montpelier. Maple sap was tap-tapping into buckets on the hill above the gold-domed State House as most of the one hundred fifty Representatives and thirty Senators hurried into the legislative halls as though there was something special about this day.

"What's all the excitement about?" asked a teacher who was leading a class to the visitors' gallery, where the public can watch and listen.

"There's going to be a vote for a law about Vermont's environment," said one of the pages, who are young people who help in the State House.

Some of the legislators explained to the students that many citizens were concerned that Vermont's way of life was being threatened by heedless growth and development, and that land ought not to be developed without first considering the effects on the environment. The bill which would be voted on was complex and original, for no other state had passed such a law before.

"It's downright radical," grumbled one person.

"It's every bit as sensible as the Vermont Constitution itself," said another. "Business interests should not be allowed to develop land in such a way that the rights of others are abused."

The bill, later known as "Act 250," passed that day and attracted the attention of the nation. Regional District Com-

missions and a State Environmental Board for appeals were
set up to rule on local developments of more than ten acres,
and to decide whether to grant permits after considering
how the venture would affect the air, water, soil, roads,
schools, scenic beauty, historic sites, and rare natural areas.

For example, if a developer wanted to build a large housing area that would contaminate a stream, that would be
unfair to other people in the community.

Vermonters have always had a tradition of loving their
land, from the Green Mountain peaks to the meadows and
bogs, so they were excited about this new bill that would
help to protect the natural benefits and beauties of their
environment.

What is Vermont's "way of life"? What kind of land does
she have? What are her people like, and why? What was
Vermont like in the very beginning? How will her people
live in the future? Such thoughts may have been in the
minds of the legislators who voted to pass "Act 250" in the
spring of 1970.

1. Indians, Frenchmen, and Englishmen

The Land

Vermont isn't very big, only 9,609 square miles. Texas, for example, is almost thirty times larger. A strong hiker could walk in a few weeks to visit Vermont's four neighbors—Canada, New Hampshire, Massachusetts, and New York.

A direct hike from Canada on the north to Massachusetts on the south is 158 miles. From New York on the west to New Hampshire on the east along the northern border is 90 miles, and along its southern border the state is 40 miles wide.

People call Vermont the Green Mountain State after the mountains that run north and south down her center like an arched backbone that appears to cut the state in half. Mount Mansfield, Vermont's highest mountain, rises 4,393 feet in the Green Mountains east of Burlington.

To the west and south of the Green Mountains lies a smaller range called the Taconic Mountains. All of Vermont's mountains are old beyond imagination, much older than the Alps of Europe or the Himalayas of Asia. Geologists, who read the earth's history in rocks, believe that the

3

mountains of Vermont were pushed up in folds, perhaps as long as three hundred million years ago, from the earth's center, just as you might squeeze up clay or dough with your hand. The mountains and deep valleys lie like the wrinkles of a crumpled rug, with rivers in the creases of the deep valleys.

Marine clay and fossils tell geologists that a salty inland sea once came in from the north as far down as Lake Champlain, and the Connecticut River valley was probably also an inland sea. In fact, the fossil of a whale's skeleton was found in Vergennes in 1849.

About one hundred thousand years ago, long after the mountains were formed, a great ice sheet came scraping and grinding down over the land like an enormous bulldozer twice as high as Vermont's highest peaks. When the ice began to melt, around twelve thousand years ago, the mountains were still there, but soil and rocks had been moved, sometimes in a topsy-turvy fashion, and lakes and rivers were cut into the earth.

"Oh, these back-breaking rocks!" farmers have always groaned as they cleared them from the fields, to make the glacier's rubble into stone walls.

Today Vermont's greatest lake, Lake Champlain, covers more than half her western border. The water of Lake Champlain flows north into the Richelieu River—and then

into the St. Lawrence River and finally into the Atlantic Ocean—so when you go north you go *down* the lake to its outlet, and when you go south you go *up* the lake to its headwaters.

The Connecticut River forms the eastern border of the state, and Lake Memphremagog lies astride the Canadian border. The area that drains into lakes or rivers is called the watershed.

Vermont has many small lakes and crystal springs that bubble out of hillsides to make trout streams and furnish cool drinking water. The great ice sheet gave Vermont something special by leaving rock excavations that in time became poorly drained lakes, which filled up with melted snow and dead leaves. After many years this turned to damp soil, making bogs where rare plants grow. Here one can find pitcher plants, orchids, lady's-slippers, rare grasses, and even plants that eat insects. There are a few rare bogs that quake, where the earth is not quite steady. Ryder Pond in Windham County is a quaking bog.

Rock collectors know that among her minerals Vermont has granite, marble, slate, talc, asbestos, limestone, and even a little gold. Pasture lands feed cattle, and birch, beech, and evergreen trees help cover her hills. Maple trees give sugar in the spring and turn the state into a red and gold fairyland in the autumn before the winter snows come. Deer, beaver, otter, grouse, osprey, and song birds are among the plentiful wild creatures that live in the state.

And the people? Who are they and where did they come from? Who were the first people in Vermont?

Archeologists, the scientific detectives who try to unravel the histories of ancient people, have discovered that Vermont once had a prehistoric civilization, mysterious and known to few people.

The Indians

In 1973 in the town of Highgate up in the northwest corner of Vermont, a backhoe operator was digging a cellar hole for a new house when he uncovered some green-stained bones. "Maybe this is the skeleton of a murdered person," he thought. "Maybe I should call the State Police."

"These bones are old. Besides, they are buried very deep, about six feet under the earth," said the puzzled police officer. "I think I'll call the State Pathologist."

When this official state doctor arrived he examined the bones. "This is an ancient burial," he declared. And he in turn called the archeologists at the University of Vermont.

The archeology professors got permission from the property owner to investigate the site. Three weeks of careful work by students, teachers, and even boys and girls of the neighborhood uncovered a large burial ground of an early Indian group who lived here about two thousand five hundred to two thousand years ago, who seem to have been related by trade or migration to the Adena people, who lived at the same period but much farther west. Experts were able to identify the bones because they were arranged in a special ceremonial fashion and covered with red ochre—a type of earth containing iron. Copper beads, which had stained the bones green, and stone tools were found with the burials.

The artifacts, the things made by the people, and the skeletons are now at the University of Vermont.

The map of the world shows that Russia and Alaska almost touch, divided only by the narrow Bering Strait. Scientists think that here there was once solid land connecting Asia and North America. Nobody knows for sure, but it is likely that Indians walked from Asia, and later moved east, some of them finally reaching Vermont. Scientists who study races realize that American Indians and Asians have many physical characteristics in common.

Although archeologists don't all agree as to the exact details of Vermont's Indian history, most scholars think that there were three periods of Indian culture. Dates can be placed by laboratory tests and sometimes by intelligent guesses.

Archeologists believe that about ten thousand years ago, when the last ice sheet had just gone away and the inland sea still covered part of the surface of Vermont, Paleo Indians, meaning the "very early Indians," lived here. The clue is that they left behind special kinds of fluted spear points that were not made by other people.

The land at that time was covered with moss like the Arctic tundra, over which caribou and herd animals wandered freely. It was not until eight thousand to four thousand years ago that forests began to grow, making fewer edible plants and less room for people and animals to roam.

Maybe that is why the Paleo Indians went away, for they disappeared and nobody knows what happened to them. Perhaps some future archeologist will solve their mystery.

They were replaced somewhat later, about six thousand to three thousand years ago, by a second group called the Archaic, meaning "old," Indians. These people lived by streams, and made stone sinkers to weight down their nets for snaring fish. They also made stone spears to throw at animals and enemies, and they even made woodworking tools to make grooves in wood, for there were now evergreen forests.

The Archaic Indians gathered herbs and roots and lived in caves or skin shelters. They made dugout canoes and seem to have traveled great distances. They made slate tools like the ones used by historic Eskimos in the Arctic.

They might even have had dogs, for dog bones have been found in their burial places. Dogs probably came from northern Asia, generations of them traveling across the world to Vermont with the Archaic Indians. The animals may have been used in hunting wild game, or for pulling sleds.

About three thousand to two thousand years ago a third group appeared here called the Woodland Indians, because by that time Vermont had woods with broad-leafed trees like the ones we have today. The people whose burial sites were found at Highgate were among the early Woodland Indians. Nobody knows for sure whether or not the Woodland Indians were descended from the Archaic Indians. This is another mystery to be solved by tomorrow's archeologists.

We know more about the Woodland group than about the older civilizations because the Woodland Indians were the people here when the first Europeans came to America less than a thousand years ago.

The Iroquois nation of Indians, who belong to the Woodland group, said that they once owned all of what is now Vermont. They tried in modern times to get the Vermont legislature to pay them for the land, but they did not succeed.

Another major nation of Indians of the Woodland group are the Algonquin, who were the most important to Vermont's history. The Algonquin and the Iroquois were enemies, and about four hundred years ago the Algonquin drove most of the Iroquois west from the Lake Champlain region.

Some of the Algonquin tribes were the Coos, who lived along the upper Connecticut River, and the Mohicans, who lived in the southwestern part of the state. But the ones we know best in Vermont are the Abnaki, who roamed the land between the Connecticut River and Lake Champlain and left at least two hundred sites, some in each of Vermont's present fourteen counties, to show where they had been.

The Abnaki usually traveled by water, in dugout or birchbark canoes. An Indian could come from Lake Champlain up Otter Creek to the stream called the Battenkill, then on to the Hudson River in New York. Or he could paddle up the Winooski River and carry his canoe a few miles over the mountains to the White River and go into the Connecticut River. There were many such Indian "roads."

By the 1600's the Abnaki, like the other Woodland Indians, used bows and arrows, something the older Indians did not know about, for hunting and warfare. They made dishes of birchbark and pottery, and some of them lived in bark houses as well as in caves and in skin-covered wigwams. Anyone who walks down the rocks by the bridge over the Connecticut River at Bellows Falls can see pictures carved in the rocks long ago by Indians.

The Abnaki even made maple syrup. How could an Indian boil sap with only clay or birchbark pots? Probably he dug a hole and lined it with skin and filled it with sap. Beside it he built a fierce fire, and in it heated rocks as hot as he could get them, and then he dropped the hot rocks into the sap. That way he heated the sap over and over until finally he had syrup. He could boil water the same way for cooking his food.

Another way to make syrup is to freeze the sap in clay pots each night and toss out the ice in the morning. If one does this enough times a thin syrup will be left in the pot.

Indians found that bits of sugar crystals formed around cuts in the maple tree's bark. Indian children licked sugar crystals just as Vermont children do today, and in birchbark cups they caught sap from the cut ends of small branches, and drank it.

When the Europeans came, probably more than 120,000 Indians were living in Vermont, more people than are in today's Burlington, Vermont's largest city. The newcomers brought diseases which Indians had never had before, and many Indians died from these sicknesses. They also died in warfare.

The Abnaki called Lake Champlain *Petowbowk,* and they thought that a certain great rock at the southern end of the lake was a guardian who must be pleased with gifts. They called it *Wojahase,* meaning "the Forbidder." Each time they passed it they would toss the rock an offering of corn. Then they felt safe, for they knew Wojahase would look after them as they traveled. If they ignored the rock, they were afraid that its spirit would come after them, yelling and groaning.

Like other Indians, the Abnaki roamed the land seeking good fishing and hunting grounds. Long before white men came to the area, Abnaki would come each summer to fish at the spot on the Connecticut River that is now Bellows Falls. Even after the town was settled, they came and built their wigwams on the land of friendly Vermonters. In the autumn of 1856 their old chief told his people to return to their winter camping grounds in Canada without him.

"I am going to the Great Spirit before many moons," he said. "Leave me here."

Sorrowfully his people left him, but his two sons stayed with their dying father. People of the town raised money to build a warm house for the chief, but he died in his wigwam before the house was finished.

Many townspeople went to his funeral, which was conducted by the local minister. The last of the Abnaki chiefs in Vermont was buried in the Rockingham Town burying ground, with no marker to show where his grave is today.

Today archeologists and students are working at Indian "digs" in a number of sites in Vermont, and alert people often find arrowheads or scraps of pottery in the ground. Recording and labeling such finds help to trace the history of Vermont's first known human inhabitants. They report their finds to the Anthropology Department at the University of Vermont.

Champlain, the Frenchman

Samuel
de Champlain

It was July on Lake Champlain in the year 1609. Waterfowl flew up from the shores with great rushes of wings; frogs jumped, fish swam away, and little animals drinking along the water's edge hung back in the grass at the intrusion.

Streaming up the lake were twenty-four canoes filled with sixty feathered and painted Indians, accompanied by three white men whose metal armor gleamed in the sunlight. Beside the white men lay long shiny guns.

The travelers looked ahead where they could see high mountain peaks.

"Snow," said one in French—for they came from France, these white men.

The leader of the expedition, whose name was Samuel de Champlain, noted in his journal that snow had been seen. Nowadays most people think that snow could not have been seen in July from Lake Champlain. Perhaps what they saw was light reflected from outcroppings of rock.

As far as we know, no white man had ever seen this lake before. Champlain was sure he was the first European to come there, so he named the lake for himself and claimed it for France.

These French explorers had come from Quebec on the St.

Lawrence River, where the French traders had made a settlement the year before. They had agreed to help their Indian friends, the Abnaki, fight their old enemies the Iroquois, some of whom lived on the banks of Lake Champlain.

The Abnaki chief in charge of the canoes held a parley with Champlain. He spoke in French, which he had learned from the explorers.

"The Iroquois will see us," the chief said. "From now on we will travel only by night."

Champlain followed the advice of the guide. Soon they met a group of Iroquois who said they wanted to fight. According to the rules of their warfare the Iroquois advanced when the enemy came ashore.

When Champlain was within thirty paces of three Iroquois chiefs who were in front, he drew his gun and fired, killing the first chief and wounding another.

Then a second Frenchman shot the third chief. The Iroquois, who had never seen firearms before, fled in terror, but the Abnaki captured a dozen prisoners. When they camped that night the Abnaki tortured the Iroquois prisoners, for that was part of their rules of warfare.

The trigger of Champlain's gun set off a reaction he was not able to control—a reaction that had results lasting for the rest of history. Indians began to fear and mistrust white men, and with their crude weapons they had no chance against the guns of the Europeans.

The Mystery of Johne Graye

Although it seems to be an established fact that Champlain was the first European to put foot in what is now Vermont, there are some mysterious speculations that Frenchmen might not after all have been the first white men to come here.

Could Vikings from Iceland have come into this land that would one day be Vermont? The Viking story is told in the sagas of Iceland, ancient stories of Norse explorers. Although there is no proof, there is at least a possibility that about the year 1000 they might have come into Lake Champlain by way of the St. Lawrence River, just as Champlain did. This is another mystery of history for someone to unravel in the future.

There is even a legend that Celtic monks from Ireland may have visited this land, even before the known Viking explorations of North America. Vermont farmers today are often puzzled by mysterious stone structures that do not appear to be of Indian or colonial origin. Some experts think that these may be related to similar structures known to have been built by these Celtic travelers of twelve hundred years ago.

Over a century ago, two men on the banks of the Missisquoi River near the Canadian border in what is now the town of Swanton found, buried in the sand, a crusty lead tube about four inches long. Puzzled, they pulled out of the tube what seemed to be an ancient piece of paper, which bore this message:

Nov. 29 AD 1564

This is the solme daye
I must now die this is
the 90th day sine we
lef the Ship all have
Perished and on the
Banks of this river
I die to [or, so] farewelle
may future Posteritye
knowe our end

X   Johne Graye

What excitement! Local men and women—and children, too—pushed in to have a look at this strange message from the past. Finally the tube and its contents were turned over to a team of experts for examination. Historians knew that there had been many unrecorded voyages to the new world in the early days. A sailor could have been shipwrecked and wandered into what is now Vermont.

Many authorities studied the document, some saying it was real, and some saying it was a forgery put there by a prankster. Tests on the ink and the paper seemed to show that it could not have been as old as the date on the message. But there are still some people who think this might be a real message from a voyager who came here before Champlain.

Today nobody seems to know where the paper and tube are, although they had been in various Vermont museums.

Father Jogues

In the 1600's most well-dressed people in Europe wore beaver-felt hats. They were the latest Paris style, and French merchants in North America found that they could get rich by trading in beaver skins. The English and Dutch, too, began trading for furs, but the French controlled the St. Lawrence River and Lake Champlain, and so they were ahead in the fur race.

At this time in the 17th Century, there was a great religious struggle going on in Europe between the Catholics and the Protestants. The King of France, Louis XIV, wanted to establish colonies in New France, as Canada was called, and since the official religion of France was Catholic, he allowed only Catholic settlers to come.

So these settlers followed the fur traders who were already in New France, and Jesuit Catholic priests came, too, to christen the new French babies and hold church services and teach catechisms. Mostly the Jesuits came to serve as missionaries to the Indians, for the French government thought that the Indians should give up their old religions and become Christians.

One of these missionaries was Father Isaac Jogues. For several years he lived with the Huron Indians of the friendly Algonquin nation, but Father Jogues yearned to convert the enemies of the Algonquin, the Iroquois. One day he was captured by the Iroquois in a bloody fight.

"My chance has come," said Father Jogues, thanking Heaven. "Now I shall have an opportunity to minister to my enemies."

The Iroquois tortured the gentle priest most horribly, but Father Jogues refused to leave although he had a chance to run away. Even when he was ransomed he wanted to go back to work with the Iroquois. Finally it was arranged that he could live with the Mohawk, a tribe of the Iroquois. On his way to his new home he camped in what would become Vermont—at Isle la Motte in Lake Champlain, and on the banks of Otter Creek.

At first, things went well with Father Jogues and the Mohawk, but when there was sickness among the people, and when caterpillars caused the crops to fail, the troubled Indians blamed the white man.

"The white father is the cause of our troubles," decided the Mohawk chiefs in tribal council. Believing that natural disasters were caused by evil spirits which acted through human sorcerers, they sentenced the priest to death, and executed him by chopping off his head.

French Settlements

French military people, wanting to expand New France, in 1666 moved into the Lake Champlain region and built Fort Ste. Anne at Isle la Motte.

"Ah, those carefree soldiers at the fort," said the people at Quebec when they heard that the young men spent their time hunting and fishing and fencing.

At that particular time there was not much fighting to occupy the three hundred or so soldiers, but within a few years disease struck, and so many men died that the fort was abandoned in 1679, ending Vermont's first white settlement.

Two hundred years later archeologists dug into mounds at the site of the fort and found old bricks from a chapel and from bakers' ovens, as well as broken dishes, nails, coins, and bits of ancient guns.

Although that fort did not last very long, the French built other forts on the lake and the King of France granted large tracts of land, called "seigneuries," to French noblemen. These landowners agreed to have their tracts settled and to govern the people who came from France to work on the land.

Old French maps show that the seigneuries extended as far south as Middlebury, but the French settlements were not a great success. In today's town of Alburg out in Lake Champlain, Windmill Point is marked as the place where in the long-ago forgotten days of 1740 a Frenchman built a windmill that is said to have cost a sum of money amounting to eight hundred dollars. Records show that he also built a church, and that settlers came there to live.

The largest of the French settlements was at Chimney Point opposite Crown Point on Lake Champlain near the old French Fort St. Frederic. With the fort as protection, for about thirty years as many as three hundred men, women, and children lived in the village, until they were driven out in 1759. When they left, the French burned all their buildings rather than let anyone else have them. Only some chimneys, outlined against the sky, remained to give Chimney Point its name.

Some people have found old artifacts deep in the earth where the village used to be; and French herbs, not native to Vermont, can be found growing among the rocks. If ghosts walk there, as the old stories say, do they whisper to each other in French?

English Settlements, the Stage for War

While the French were slowly moving south from Canada to explore, to claim land, and to settle around Lake Champlain, other nations were not idle. In 1620, just eleven years after Samuel de Champlain took his canoe into Lake Champlain, the Pilgrims, who were English, sailed their ship, the *Mayflower*, into Plymouth Bay in Massachusetts to begin a settlement there.

The English kings and queens wanted North America settled for England, and other groups of Englishmen soon followed the Pilgrims. For more than a century afterward, English rulers granted large tracts of land with vague boundaries to friends who brought colonists to settle in New England. However, England never established a colony in Vermont, as she did in Massachusetts, Connecticut, and New York. In fact, in the early 1600's some of Vermont was claimed by the Dutch, who had established New Netherlands in an area along the Hudson River. The land that would one day be Vermont was wild and uncharted except for the Lake Champlain region, which France said belonged to her.

By the late 1600's the English people had made settlements on the Connecticut River as far north as today's Northfield, Massachusetts, but although these communities were protected by stockades, they were destroyed by Indians again and again. The French and their allies, the Abnaki Indians, were enemies of the English settlers because England and France were at war and both nations wanted to control North America. Between the English and the French lay the area we call Vermont.

"This is our land," said the French governors, looking south from Canada.

"This is our land," said the English leaders, looking north from Massachusetts.

"This is our land," said the Iroquois and Abnaki, looking angrily at each other—and looking fearfully at the Europeans who were squeezing in from both sides.

Obviously a major fight was brewing. Called the French and Indian wars (for there were actually four periods of fighting with temporary peace in between), the struggle between the French and the English and each side's Indian allies shook North America for nearly a century, from 1689 to 1760.

We know about the French forts and small settlements around Lake Champlain. But what was happening to the English people who were trying to move their frontier north toward present-day Vermont?

War and Captives

The French and Indian wars were fought on land and sea, and in Indian raids against the settlers on the frontier. The French used the Abnaki for allies to massacre the English, and told them that the English were wicked people who should be driven out. The English in turn tried to influence the Iroquois to scalp and murder the French and chase them away from Lake Champlain and Canada.

Kidnapped English captives were marched to Canada and held prisoner until friends and relatives could raise enough money to buy them back. Sometimes it took a long time to arrange this ransom, because it was hard to get messages back and forth.

On the long marches to Canada each prisoner had a special Indian assigned to him to be a father, mother, brother, or sister. The Indian "relatives" guarded their prisoners and saw that they were fed and sheltered and kept healthy. Some captives and their special Indians became close friends when they began to know each other as human beings, and kept in touch with each other for the rest of their lives.

In 1704 there was a frontier English settlement in Deerfield in Massachusetts only a few miles from Vermont's present border. Indians attacked and burned Deerfield and took one hundred nineteen prisoners, having first killed forty-seven settlers. The prisoners were forced by their captors to walk north through wild country to Montreal, about three hundred miles away.

Among the prisoners was the Reverend John Williams, who later wrote a book called *The Redeemed Captive* in which he told of his experiences as a prisoner. Many died on the journey. On March 5, 1704, the prisoners stopped in what is now the town of Rockingham in Windham County, and there Mr. Williams preached the first Protestant sermon in Vermont. The poor fellow's wife and baby had just died on the march, and his other children were separated from him, but he had the courage to conduct a service of worship in the woods.

When English prisoners were taken to Canada, the priests wanted to convert them to the Catholic faith. Old records show that many did become Catholics. Mr. Williams made up his mind that his charges from Deerfield would not lose their Protestant religion, but his own son and daughter became Catholics. His eight-year-old daughter, Eunice, never returned home to live but stayed on with the Indians and grew up with them as one of the tribe. However, many of the Deerfield captives were ransomed and got home the next year.

Fort Dummer

"We need some more forts to stop all this kidnapping and raiding," fumed William Dummer, the acting Governor of Massachusetts, in 1724. There had already been countless Indian raids and there were sure to be more, so Fort Dummer was built on the banks of the Connecticut River in 1724 on the outskirts of what is Brattleboro today.

Lieutenant Timothy Dwight and twelve soldiers built it with the help of four carpenters in the cold month of February. The carpenters were paid five shillings a day except for

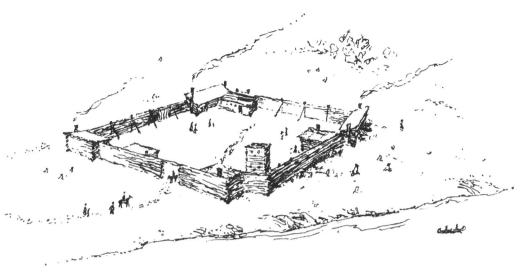

an Indian carpenter, Johnny Crowfoot, who was paid six shillings a day, good wages in those times.

"He deserves the extra pay," said the other carpenters. "He works harder than we do and does better work."

Soon fifty-five English soldiers came to live at Fort Dummer, along with their families and some Indians. In 1726 the Dwights had a baby boy named Timothy, who is believed to be the first English child born in Vermont.

Little Timothy smiled at the Indians who lived and worked around the fort as he lay on a blanket by the river where his mother did her washing with the other women.

Massachusetts officials tried to be friendly with the local Indians, and built a trading post where the Indians from many groups could come to trade their furs. Captain Dwight, as he was now called, caused Indians to be employed as soldiers, including three sachems, or chiefs. Some English people were worried that too much whiskey was traded to the Indians, and a chaplain was sent to try to convert the Indians to Christianity, but most of the Indians liked their own religion better.

The Dwight family left, but Fort Dummer continued for a while to be an important fighting and trading post in the wilderness.

More Captives

The English were half scared to death of the French and Indians, so they built more forts, including a famous one on the Connecticut River at Charlestown, New Hampshire, that was called simply "Number Four" because it was the fourth fort on the river. In August of 1754, near the time the English attacked the French village at Chimney Point, a family was kidnapped from Fort Number Four.

Mr. and Mrs. Johnson, their three children, and Mrs. Johnson's sister were routed out of bed, when they were all asleep just before daylight, by yelling Indians. They were permitted to put on a few clothes and without more ado they were herded in line and headed for Canada.

Many years later, Mrs. Johnson wrote a book called *The Captivity of Mrs. Johnson,* and in it she described the march:

"When the time came for us to prepare to march I almost expired at the thought . . . to travel through a dismal forest with three small children, the eldest Sylvanus, who was but six years old. My eldest daughter, Susannah, was four and Polly the other, two. My husband was barefoot."

Mrs. Johnson lost one shoe, but she had an even greater difficulty. She was about to give birth to a baby, and on the second day of the march, a chilly, rainy day, her daughter was born in a hut of boughs made by the Indian women. She named the new baby Captive.

Today on the outskirts of Felchville in Windsor County there is an old marker that tells the story and marks the site where little Captive was born.

The Indian women made gifts for the baby prisoner, and when the group reached a French fort on Lake Champlain the French ladies were kind to the new mother. They put her to bed and dressed the baby in Parisian clothes and played with her like a doll amid laughter and gay chatter. She was a healthy baby who grew up and became a valuable citizen. This family all survived and returned home.

There were many other stories of prisoners, of bravery, sorrow, and separations. Mrs. Jemima Sartwell Howe was taken prisoner by the Indians at Bridgman's Fort in the present town of Vernon. Mr. Howe was killed, and his grave can be seen today, marked by a slate stone on which his name is spelled "How." His wife and seven children were marched through the Vermont wilderness to Canada.

Called "the fair captive," for she was very beautiful, she was separated from her children and suffered great trials. In spite of that, Mrs. Howe said the Indians were personally kind to her, and she was able to report in later years, "For such savage masters, in such indigent circumstances, we could not rationally hope for kinder treatment than we received."

Records show that there were 1,196 English settlers captured and taken to Canada from New England during the French and Indian wars.

Rogers' Rangers and Indian Fighting

When Robert Rogers was a boy in about 1740, he helped his father and brothers build a house on the frontier.

"I'm so tired I could die," said one of his brothers, pausing to rest.

Robert hurt in every muscle, but he kept on cutting trees, hauling stones, and digging the cellar hole. "We can't stop now," he said. "We're going to have a house and clear the land for a farm and not be so poor any more."

The house was finished at last, the pride of the Rogers family. And then the Indians came yelling from the forest, faces painted and waving tomahawks, and they burned the house. Teenager Robert swore to avenge this by fighting Indians when he got older.

Robert Rogers became the head of a group of rangers, as companies of Indian-fighters were called. A great woodsman, Robert Rogers was afraid of nothing and nobody, and his anger at the Indians burned like a steady flame. Under their fierce leader Rogers' Rangers became the most famous of all the many companies of men who banded together to protect the frontier.

Rogers' Rangers helped the British Army in the last days of the French and Indian wars. When Rogers was ordered to wipe out an Indian village on the Missisquoi River near the present town of Swanton he did just that. He and his men killed two hundred St. Francis Indians, a group made up of remnants of Algonquin tribes, and set free some white prisoners in a bloody shoot-out. It made the frontier safer for the English, but it was a black day for the Indians.

Chief Greylock

A St. Francis Indian who hated the whites as much as Rogers hated the Indians was Chief Greylock, a fearless warrior who, like Robert Rogers, was afraid of nothing and nobody. For more than half a century after 1700 he terrified the English.

He had a castle, as Indian villages were sometimes called, somewhere on the shore of Missisquoi Bay, and Indian-fighters tried in vain to capture him. Other Englishmen tried to

please him with gifts and bribes, but Greylock refused to come to terms with the people he felt had stolen his lands and brought sorrow to his people. This brave Indian never surrendered. Nobody knows for sure where or when he died, but it was probably shortly before the end of the French and Indian wars.

Victory for England

In 1758, Major General James Abercromby led a mighty British force sailing down Lake Champlain with flags flying and bands playing. The French, under General Louis Joseph de Montcalm, waited for them at Fort Carillon, later to be renamed Fort Ticonderoga. The British general made so many blunders and lost so many of his finest soldiers that he was badly beaten and recalled. His angry troops nicknamed him "Aunt Nabby Cromby."

Then the British government sent Major General Jeffery Amherst to lead the fighting in North America. He seized the French forts on Lake Champlain, and in 1760 he had his soldiers build the Crown Point Military Road over the Green Mountains to connect Fort Ticonderoga on Lake Champlain with Fort Number Four on the Connecticut River.

"What rich land," said one soldier to another as they cut the trees through the forest.

"When this war is over I'm coming here to stake out a farm," said another as the road neared completion.

Finally, Quebec was captured by the English in September of 1759. General James Wolfe, a popular British officer, found a secret path that led to the city. General Montcalm, the French commander who was equally well liked by his troops, defended the city nobly. The English won the battle, but in the final bloody fight both generals were killed.

The war was soon over, for General Amherst captured Montreal in September of 1760, and all of Canada surrendered.

When the Treaty of Paris was signed in 1763, England got most of North America, but many French people continued to live in Canada.

2. The New Hampshire Grants, New York, and Ethan Allen

Benning Wentworth

While all the fighting between England and France was going on, some changes were made in New Hampshire and Massachusetts. In the beginning, New Hampshire had been part of Massachusetts, with a Lieutenant Governor who was responsible to the Governor of Massachusetts. One of these Lieutenant-Governors was rich and powerful John Wentworth, whose son Benning was born in Portsmouth, New Hampshire.

Benning was such a brash little boy that his father's friend Governor Belcher of Massachusetts said the child had "pertness" and "insolence of manners." Benning graduated from Harvard College and went into the shipping business with his father.

Then troubles overtook Benning. His father died and the business failed, due to the wars that were being fought in Europe as well as in North America. The time came when Benning was about to be put in prison for debt, as was the custom in those days.

But one of the men to whom Benning Wentworth owed a lot of money said, "Well, I won't get my money back with that young man lying in jail. He has brains. Why not get him out of this scrape, so he can get to work and pay back the money he owes? But how can we do this?"

The other creditors thought hard and deeply. "Why not make him Governor of New Hampshire?" said one. "After all, his father was Lieutenant Governor. We can persuade the King to make New Hampshire into a separate colony, and if a man as smart as Benning Wentworth can't make that job pay off, then I don't deserve to get my money back."

And this is exactly what happened. By a considerable amount of pulling strings, New Hampshire was taken away from the colony of Massachusetts, and Benning Wentworth became its first Governor. So instead of being in jail on January 14, 1741, young Mr. Wentworth was inaugurated as Governor. The first thing he did was ask for a salary. In those years governors were not paid for doing their job, so this was a new idea. And then he looked around to see where he could make the most money to pay off his debts, and avoid being whisked from the governor's chair to jail.

GOV. BENNING WENTWORTH

Looking westward from Portsmouth on the crude map, he saw the uncharted lands beyond the Connecticut River. "Ah," he said to himself, "this land might belong to New Hampshire. In fact, I'm sure it does, all the way to this line twenty miles east of the Hudson River, and the King has just declared a firm boundary here on the south between New Hampshire and Massachusetts. Why don't I divide this wil-

derness into townships about the usual six miles square—
that's a handy size—and sell it very cheaply. It will take a
few years to get it rolling, but it will pay off richly in fees.
I'll reserve a bit of land for myself in each grant, too." And
he rubbed his hands, thinking joyfully of riches to come.

True, Indian warfare was still a threat in spite of periods
of peace. But the war would end eventually, and people
would want new lands to settle because population was rising in New England. Shrewd men who had money to invest
realized that this was a good risk. New York seemed to have
a claim on the land, but in 1749, when Governor Wentworth
first put the land up for sale, New York didn't make much
effort to stop the activity in the New Hampshire Grants, as
the region soon came to be known. Governor Wentworth sat
back and began to sell land, and before long he was piling
up money.

Bennington was the first town to be sold, and the Governor named it for himself. In the next fifteen years he granted,
or sold, land for one hundred thirty-eight towns to be settled. He got as rich as an Arabian prince, for in each town he
held back some land for himself, which became more valuable as the towns were settled.

Samuel Robinson from Hardwick, Massachusetts, a soldier
in the French and Indian wars, passed through the town of
Bennington on his way home from Canada in 1761.

"Now that we are going to have peace with France," he
said aloud to the great forest about him, "this would be a
good place to live. I could clear this beautiful land and make
a fine farm for my family."

When he got home he gathered some friends and relatives
about him and persuaded six families to come settle in Bennington with him. Soon there were forty families there—

men, women, and children eager for a new home in the wilderness.

Many a soldier from the wars, walking home on the new military roads or Indian trails, had the same idea about other towns. Investors who had bought up the grants began to advertise in newspapers to promote sales of smaller parcels in the hills and valleys of what would some day be Vermont.

Meanwhile, Benning Wentworth paid off his debts and built himself a great house that is still standing today, open to the public, in Portsmouth, New Hampshire. On his sixtieth birthday, when he was a lonely widower, he had a lavish party to which he invited all the rich and powerful people in the town. He asked the Episcopal minister to sit by his side.

On his staff of servants was twenty-year-old Martha Hilton, who had worked as a maid in his house ever since she was fifteen. When dinner was over, Governor Wentworth clapped his hands for the servants to take away the dishes. Then, to the surprise of the guests, the door was flung open and into the room stepped a beautiful young woman, dressed in the latest style.

"Mr. Brown," said the Governor to the minister, "would you perform a wedding ceremony in the presence of this company?"

A gasp went around the room as Martha, the serving maid who had turned into an elegant lady, became Mrs. Benning Wentworth. As far as history records, the bride and groom lived happily ever after. The poet Longfellow wrote of this wedding in his poem "Lady Wentworth."

New York Steps In

Soon settlers were piling household goods on oxen or their own backs and heading north mostly from Connecticut and Massachusetts, whistling and singing as they trudged along to their new homes in the wilderness. The towns which would soon be settled were planned, with obligations placed on the landowners. Bennington, whose grant was typical, required that every owner must cultivate five acres out of every fifty acres within the first five years of ownership, and must continue to improve the land. Land-clearing was terribly hard work, and would use all the muscles of all the men, women, and children.

Land was reserved to rent for money to support a school, a church, and the minister, and a plan was set up for each town to govern itself, with selectmen and other officials chosen by vote of the menfolk at the yearly town meeting.

In 1762 there were about fifty families settled around Bennington, and many of the people, especially around nearby Arlington, came from Litchfield County in Connecticut. Settlers around Manchester came mostly from New York, and there were even Dutch settlers in Pownal under a New York "patent," as the New York land grants were called.

Over on the Connecticut River seventy families in twelve towns, mostly from Massachusetts and Connecticut, had settled as far north as Newbury.

And then one day the acting Governor of New York, Mr. Cadwallader Colden, a Scotsman with a keen mind who had granted a few patents himself, looked east across the Hudson River and got mad.

"That rascal is selling my land!" he fumed. "I'll put a stop to that. Of course New York owns all the land west of the Connecticut River. No doubt about it."

So in 1763 Governor Colden asked King George III of England, who had recently come to the throne, to settle the matter. The King and his advisers thought it over and decided that New York did indeed own the land, and that New Hampshire must stop selling grants in it.

Governor Colden was delighted. "Aha!" he said. "I believe this means that the settlers in the New Hampshire Grants will have to pay me for this land, which they have already settled."

By now the settlers had carved their precious acres out of the forests by cutting trees and hauling rocks and pulling stumps, working as hard as people can to make a home. There were no newspapers on the frontier then, but word spread from settler to settler that they might lose their land if they did not pay again.

There were only about a thousand people in the Grants by 1765, and many of them got mad, as mad as weary, strong, adventurous, poor people can get. Fighting mad, that is. It was their land, and they weren't going to pay New York a penny, and they weren't budging. Of course, some did pay New York, but they grumbled mightily.

When New York surveyors turned up in Bennington in 1765, the settlers, and also some land speculators, decided to tell their side of it to the King. They had bought the land in good faith from a grant made by Benning Wentworth, a representative of the King, and they petitioned the King to stand behind their right to own it.

Samuel Robinson, Bennington's first settler, took the petition to England himself, a long voyage in a sailing ship. Poor Mr. Robinson died in England of the smallpox, a disease that killed many people in these bygone days, but he succeeded in getting the paper to the King's attention first. The British government ordered the Governor of New York not to bother the people in the Grants anymore.

Governor Colden was so angry, especially at the land speculators, that he defied the King and issued six hundred thousand acres in New York patents, much of it on land already owned under New Hampshire grants. By now some of the settlers were scared of the power of New York and paid the "quit rent" fee, but most of the farmers, feeling that the King was on their side and not having any money anyhow, got ready to fight.

The men got out their guns and the boys cut big sticks, and they dared New York surveyors to set foot on their land. And the pioneer women who could shoot a gun as well as the man in the house stood ready, too.

James Breakenridge of Bennington had a farm right on the New York border. One day he and sixty of his friends were harvesting corn when New York surveyors came in to throw him off his land. The farmers, who were warned and armed, ran the surveyors off with threats and shouts, and soon Mr. Breakenridge and some others who had stood up for their land were ordered to appear in court in Albany, New York.

Even in those days it cost a lot of money to hire a lawyer, so a fund was raised to help out the accused, who were poor people. However, land speculators from Connecticut were willing to contribute.

"We need someone to take charge of this," said the men of the town as they hotly discussed the injustice over their drinks of rum or beer at the Catamount Tavern in Bennington.

"How about our old Connecticut neighbor from Salisbury, Ethan Allen? He's sold his ironworks there, and seems to be at loose ends."

"Why, Ethan's the very person!" cried another man, slapping the table with excitement. "He's been up here now and again to look about. He likes this frontier life and doesn't like staying at home."

"Ethan's smart. He's just the one to head up a fight," they all agreed. "Hear, hear! Let's get Ethan."

A Man Named Ethan Allen

And so it was that in May of 1770 Ethan Allen, a thirty-three-year-old farmer and businessman, said goodbye to his wife and children, whom he left on a Massachusetts farm near his old Connecticut home, and set out for Bennington. Years before, Ethan's dreams of going to college had blown away when his father had died leaving teenage Ethan to look after his mother and his seven younger brothers and sisters. But Ethan was a reading lad, and he kept right on learning and stretching his mind and answering every challenge that came his way. The invitation from Bennington was such a challenge.

CATAMOUNT TAVERN

When he arrived at the Catamount Tavern he heard indignant stories of the high-handed "Yorkers" who tried to take over honest men's farms, and then arrested them for rioting if they resisted. The stories got more and more exaggerated as the night wore on.

"First, I'll go to New Hampshire and get the Governor to give me the original land certificates," said Ethan Allen grandly. "Then I'll get the best lawyer in New England, and we'll see who can run folks off their own land." There were shouts of assent. Everybody felt good to have swaggering, confident Ethan Allen take over.

Ethan Allen got on his horse the very next day and set out on the one hundred fifty miles of rugged trails to Portsmouth, New Hampshire, to see the new Governor, John Wentworth, Benning's nephew. John Wentworth was not much interested in the plight of the people in the Grants, but he gave Ethan the papers certifying that the land had been granted to the owners.

"His price will come high, but Jared Ingersoll of New Haven, Connecticut, is the best lawyer you can hire," advised the Governor, rising.

Ethan thanked His Excellency with a bow. "We'll raise the money," he said jauntily, and set off for New Haven to find Mr. Ingersoll. If only he could persuade this lawyer to take the case they could impress the haughty New York court with their superior ability.

And Ethan did get Jared Ingersoll to defend the settlers when the trials opened in Albany in June of 1770. By then, Ethan had traveled more than four hundred miles and bought a bit of Grants land himself.

The first case was against Isaiah Carpenter who in 1765 had bought a farm at Shaftsbury, near Bennington, and had farmed it for five years. In 1769 Governor Colden had granted the same land to a Major Small, who got a posse of Yorkers to run Carpenter off the land, and the new "owner" moved in. But soon the angry neighbors were so threatening that the Major ran away in fright and complained to Governor Colden.

As soon as the trial opened, Small's lawyer said that he did not think Carpenter's deed from old Governor Wentworth should be considered "admissible evidence," meaning that he thought the sale was no good, and the New York judge agreed.

Because these bills of sale or grants were the basis for Lawyer Ingersoll's case, he and Ethan Allen angrily walked out, shouting to the world that the court was unfair and prejudiced. It turned out that the New York judge had also bought some New York patents in Vermont himself, and stood to profit by this decision.

Ethan Allen put up at an Albany inn for the night, and before he left town the New York lawyers dropped by to see him.

"We can reward you with money or land if you will persuade your friends to go along with New York's decision," they whispered, according to Ethan's report later. After all, they asked, what could a few backwoods farmers hope to gain by fighting the mighty court of New York?

Ethan looked at them with contempt. "The gods of the hills are not the gods of the valley," he replied.

"What does that mean?" asked one of the lawyers.

"If you will accompany me to the hills of Bennington you will see," said Ethan defiantly.

The Green Mountain Boys

The legal battle was over, but the fight had just begun. As soon as Ethan got back from the rigged trial in Albany in the summer of 1770, one hundred men of the Bennington area got together at the Catamount Tavern to set up a Committee of Safety.

"All right, we tried to fight it out legally, now we'll use force," shouted one man.

"Aye, clubs and guns," cried one of the Fay boys who was helping his father, Captain Stephen Fay, the landlord of the tavern, serve the crowd of thirsty men.

"Order, order!" pounded Dr. Jonas Fay, another son of the landlord. "We need to organize a company of volunteers to fight this together."

"Ethan Allen is our man. He'll be our leader," came the shouts from all sides.

"This was bold stroke of a hundred men," wrote Ira Allen, youngest brother of Ethan, many years later. Ethan was chosen Colonel Commandant and his cousins Seth Warner and Remember Baker, and his friends Robert Cochran and Gideon Warner and several others were appointed captains. And everybody wanted to volunteer to fight any Yorkers who tried to drive citizens off their own property.

When the Governor of New York heard about the doings at Fay's Catamount Tavern he snorted, "I'll drive that rag-tail mob back into the Green Mountains."

Ethan Allen and some of his minutemen volunteers who were congregated at the Catamount roared with laughter when the Governor's threat was reported to them. "We'll call ourselves the Green Mountain Boys," cried Ethan.

Although the Green Mountain Boys had no uniforms they all wore sprigs of evergreen in their hatbands. The companies drilled often in various towns, always on the alert for any Yorkers who might attempt to run survey-lines or kidnap settlers or try to take over farms. Any frightened settler who agreed to pay the New York fee would be banished, they decided. It would be a case of sticking together.

Ethan Allen was a giant of a man with a deep voice and great strength and wit. He carried a sword and as his mark of command he wore gold braid and epaulettes on the shoulders of his coat. There is no portrait of him, and of course there were no photographs in those days, so we have to rely on what other people said of him and use our imaginations.

Colonel Allen took charge of raising money and getting support from friends in Massachusetts and Connecticut, and he wrote stirring letters to newspapers about their problem with New York.

The *Connecticut Courant,* the newspaper that was most often read in the Grants, published things by and about Ethan Allen, and can still be seen today on microfilm. Newspapers were so rare in those days that if one copy came to the area people would gather to read it, not missing a word.

As news of the situation spread, angry people drew up petitions to the King of England, and His Majesty responded in 1772 by telling New York again to stop trying to take the settlers' land. Meanwhile there was constant scrapping between the Grants people and the Yorkers. The Green Mountain Boys were proud that they never killed a person, but they played some rough pranks on New York sheriffs and other meddlers who bothered the local people.

Mr. Breakenridge, who had had trouble before with the New York sheriff, was working in his fields one July day in 1771 when a breathless neighbor ran in with the news that about six hundred Yorkers were on the horizon. Breakenridge sent his children to alert the Green Mountain Boys, and soon about one hundred of them came to the rescue, armed.

"The first eighteen of you go in the house and barricade the doors," ordered Colonel Allen. "Raise the red flag if you need help. Now the rest of you go hide behind those hills by the road!"

When Ethan revealed his plans, the minutemen began to chuckle. At the entry of the Breakenridge farm were posted six men who, when the posse arrived, invited the Yorkers to go talk with Breakenridge at his house. At Ethan's signal the men behind the hills raised their muskets with their hats hung on the tips. Then the Yorkers realized they had been ambushed, and were surrounded by Green Mountain Boys who were safe behind the hills and in the house.

Thoroughly frightened, the Yorkers could do nothing but

run, and the Green Mountain Boys let them go with shouts of warning to stay off their land.

One night not long afterward, Sheriff John Munro tried to kidnap Remember Baker of Arlington, one of the captains of the Green Mountain Boys. Baker and his wife and son were awakened by a gang of Yorkers bursting in their door. Baker ran for his gun above the fireplace, but it was gone—apparently stolen. He grabbed his ax and began whacking at the intruders, but he was overpowered. So, ax in hand, he leaped to the ladder that led to the loft and chopped a hole in the roof. With the March snow still high against the house he jumped safely to the ground and ran for help in his nightshirt.

"There he goes—catch him!" shouted one of the kidnappers.

Poor Baker, cursing and groaning and stuck in the deep snow, was seized, and in the fight somebody cut off his thumb. In the meantime, Mrs. Baker and her son escaped through the roof hole and found help. Within an hour the Green Mountain Boys were gathered and riding to rescue Remember, whom they overtook halfway to Albany.

In the fight they got Baker and captured the sheriff, and the posse fled. They let the sheriff go, for Remember was bleeding so badly that they had to get him to the Catamount Tavern, where Dr. Fay sewed up his wound. The next day Baker went home, but without his thumb.

Seth Warner, who was Remember's cousin and friend, was so angry about this that he went to Sheriff Munro's house, hoping to find Baker's rifle there and to steal it back. The two men got into a terrible fight, and after Warner knocked Munro senseless with his sword, he went into Munro's house, found the gun, and calmly returned it to its rightful owner.

Over in New York the Governor was furious at Warner and offered rewards for the capture of some of the Green Mountain Boys. He also made a list of "rioters," who were any people who resisted New York. The Green Mountain Boys thought this was terribly funny, and nobody in the Grants would turn one of them in for any amount of money.

Said Ethan: "By virtue of a late law in the Province [of New York] they are not allowed to hang any man until they have ketched him."

In fact, Ethan Allen, Remember Baker, and Robert Cochran decided to put a price on the heads of Yorkers James Duane and John Kempe, two lawyers who had caused them a great deal of trouble, and everybody chuckled over that.

Ethan Allen and his brother Ira and some of their relatives and friends began to buy land on the Onion (now Winooski) River. Finally the Onion River Company owned one hundred ten square miles in the Champlain region. Now that the Allens were landholders under grants from New Hampshire, there was even more reason for them to fight the Yorkers who were claiming the same land.

The tricks of the Green Mountain Boys made Grants people laugh and made Yorkers tremble. To punish a Yorker sympathizer, Dr. Samuel Adams of Bennington, they tied him to a chair and hoisted him to a pole to the height of the tavern sign, which was a stuffed catamount that kept a snarling face turned toward New York. The red-faced doctor was kept dangling twenty feet in the air while townspeople, from bad little boys to proper old ladies, had a good laugh.

"What will they do next?" gasped one housewife, wiping tears of laughter from her eyes. "The latest is that they dressed themselves like Indians and ran off Surveyor Cockburn."

They scared people half to death with curses, and

whipped some bare bottoms with beech twigs, in what they called their "beech seal treatment." It was all very undignified, but without resorting to killing, they kept Yorkers from seizing their land.

When the Governor of New York increased the rewards for these pranksters, legends say that Ethan boldly rode down the streets of Albany right under the noses of the authorities, but even there nobody would turn him in.

Life in the Grants

Meanwhile the settlements were growing. In 1771, just a year after the Green Mountain Boys were organized, 4,669 people were living in the Grants; five years later, in 1776, there were twenty thousand people living in the area that would soon become the State of Vermont.

Newspapers read by the people in the Grants advertised knives and forks, colored threads, jewelry, tea, woolen material, ladies' shoes, and writing paper. Slaves were for sale in Connecticut. People read about the doings of lords and ladies in England along with serious letters about the rights of colonists. Nails were being manufactured in Quebec, it was noted, and writers who signed fancy fictitious names wrote to the papers to complain openly of British treatment of the colonies.

Schools taught reading, spelling, ciphering, and the rules of music. Most schooling was for a year or so of learning to read and write, followed by an apprenticeship for printing, hatmaking, saddlemaking, and such trades. Many song books were for sale. Both children and wives often ran away, and some families advertised lovingly in the papers asking Sarah or Tom or Prudence to please come home.

In colonial days in America smallpox, a disease almost nonexistent today, sometimes killed entire families. Even when a vaccine was discovered for preventing the disease, vaccinations were illegal in some places, including Connecticut. When Ethan Allen was a young man he had a vaccination even though it was against the law, but by the time the Grants were being settled doctors were advertising inoculations, and many daring settlers took advantage of this.

There were crimes, too, in the old days. A woman poisoned her husband; somebody counterfeited money; children were kidnapped. Two English men were hanged for killing an Indian woman. Many notices for cheap land and meetings of owners of Grants lands were advertised. Here is an advertisement by Ethan Allen's brother Levi:

THE CONNECTICUT COURANT, *Nov. 21, 1774*
LEVI ALLEN
Begs leave to acquaint the public that he has a tract of land six miles square lying on the east side Lake Champlain, north of Onion River adjoining on the water. This land has a smooth surface, fine rich soil, pure healthy air, free from stones, no high mountains in the whole tract, the Lake and the streams that empty into it abounding with divers kinds of good fish; there is a number of good homes farmers already purchased of me and some already settled on said land, and many more that viewed the same and like it well, and have contracted with me to go and settle there next spring, any inclining to purchase, may have 500 acres or more at a very moderate lay—For particulars inquire of the subscriber at Salisbury, or of Ira Allen on the premises or of Col. Thomas Chittenden, at Onion River.

[signed] LEVI ALLEN

Many plots of land were bought sight unseen by Massachusetts and Connecticut people. Usually the father would come first, traveling late in the winter while the frozen streams could be crossed easily. As soon as he could, he cleared a bit of land and threw up some kind of shelter of crude logs and boughs. Then he would go back and get his family, which in those days usually was a large one. Children worked, sun up to sun down; and "girls worked like mules," one early traveler commented.

The Tale of Ann Story

In September of 1774 Amos Story and his fourteen-year-old son, Solomon, set out for land they had bought in Salisbury, north of Rutland. Axes in hand and packs on their backs they hurried through the wilderness, for they wanted to build a cabin and bring the rest of the family to the new home before snow came.

Meanwhile, Mrs. Ann Story and the four younger children were waiting impatiently in Rutland. Ann Story was big-boned and clever with an ax, and had already learned to shoot a gun as well as any man. She could hardly wait to move to the frontier where, it turned out, she would be the first woman in the town.

"The cabin is nearly finished," said Amos. "You stay here today, Solomon, and begin to move the rocks yonder, and I will go and cut one more big tree for the few more logs we need."

When his father failed to return from his logging, Solomon went to seek him. Horrified, he found his father pinned under the fallen tree. No matter how hard he tried, the slender boy could not move the heavy tree. Finally he cut it to move it off his father, but Amos Story died.

Heartbroken and stunned, Solomon walked to Rutland to break the news to his mother. Ann Story was even braver

than people knew. That night she gathered her children about her.

"Your father and I planned this new home together," she said. "We can still have it if we all work hard."

"The Widow Story is daft," said people, shaking their heads. "No woman can live in the wilderness without a husband."

But the next February, Ann Story moved into the nearly completed cabin with her two sons and three daughters. Hostile Indians, wolves, and bears were everyday matters to them as they worked day and night to clear the land and ward off starvation.

Hard work was not the only challenge that faced this family. Several years later when the Revolutionary War brought the British marching and marauding in the neighborhood, the Story family refused to leave in spite of warnings. Ann Story dug a cave in the banks of nearby Otter Creek and hid herself and the children there until danger seemed to be past.

Then Indians came and burned her house. "I won't give up," said Ann Story with tight lips and her head held high. So with her children to help her she began all over and rebuilt the house.

The Westminster "Massacre"

Brave pioneers like the Story family clung to their land and established towns on both the east and west sides of the Green Mountains. However, there were few roads and travel over the mountains was extremely difficult, so the two sections did not know each other very well. Because the settlements on the Connecticut River were farther away from the

New York border, many of those people did not understand why the west-siders were so angry with the Yorkers.

"That Ethan Allen stirs up trouble. He's a cursing, godless man," east-side people said of him.

"Gol-durned Tories," muttered the people on the western side of the mountains about the people near the Connecticut River.

At first, even the people around Bennington didn't object to New York's government in the Grants so long as their land ownership was not questioned. But news of the land problems traveled, and one day Nathan Stone strode into the courthouse in the east-side town of Chester and shouted defiantly that the New York court could not convene there; then John Grout, a lawyer who disagreed with Stone, was driven out of town. Such friction worried the Yorker judges, so they moved the court even farther east to Westminster, which became a lively place.

It was not that the settlers did not want courts—they did want them. Most of the people were in debt for their land, and the court was the place where quarrels about debts were settled. Of course, they realized that a society could not exist without some sort of judge in charge. But what they wanted were courts that would not be biased in favor of Yorkers' claims to the land.

In 1774 the people all over the Grants were boiling about many matters. The Bennington people were quarreling with New York about land problems, and now the people around Westminster were fuming about the New York court. At the same time the people in both areas were getting daily more angry at King George III. In September of 1774 the Continental Congress met in Philadelphia to protest some of the acts of the English government.

GEORGE III

The people of Westminster met in October of 1774 and

decided to support the Continental Congress, even though Vermont was not actually a colony itself. A week or so later Leonard Spaulding of Dummerston was arrested and jailed for saying rude things about the King, upon which his friends broke into the jail and let him out. Lawlessness was in the air.

On March 14, 1775, the court was scheduled to meet again in Westminster. So many people were so angry at the New York officials that "forty good and true men" went to the judge in February and warned him that there was mighty trouble brewing.

"The sheriff is rounding up New York sympathizers, and that's going to cause a fight," said one of them. "There might be shooting."

Judge Thomas Chandler, who was a well-liked man, thought this over for a minute. "I have to convene the court," he said, "because there's a murder case that has to be tried. But I'll come a day early and see that things go peaceably."

The Yorkers and the English sympathizers were called the Court Party, and they called the anti-Yorkers the "Mob." Dr. Reuben Jones left a record of what happened in Westminster in the spring of 1775.

Because it was rumored that the Court Party was planning to take possession of the courthouse, their opponents decided to beat them to it: therefore on Monday afternoon, March 13, 1775, around one hundred anti-Yorker men simply walked in and took over the building. About an hour later the sheriff showed up with a posse which included many of the Court Party.

"Get out of there, you ruffians!" yelled the sheriff, brandishing his gun.

Dr. Jones wrote: "But we, in the house, had not any weapons of war among us, and we were determined that they should not come in with their weapons of war, except by the force of them."

Heads poked out of the windows. There were shouts and catcalls and curses from both sides. And then the sheriff read the King's proclamation for opening the court, and shouted that if the people in the building didn't get out in fifteen minutes, he would "blow a lane through them."

Curses and threats flew back and forth. The people in the building said the King's men could come in if they would leave their guns outside. Things were at a standstill when the judge arrived. "You people go home now," he told the sheriff and his men. Then he promised the men in the courthouse that there would be no guns at court and that they could stay safely in the building.

So people went home or went to the tavern, and only a few of the anti-Yorkers stayed to guard the building. Most of them were asleep when at about midnight the sentries heard a commotion. The sheriff and members of the Court Party, carrying pine torches to light their way, had come marching back.

"We'll shoot the rascals out," shouted someone from outside the building.

"Fire!" commanded the sheriff, and with that order guns were fired into the building. Then, yelling and cursing, the

sheriff's men rushed in with swords drawn, and began beating up the startled men inside.

Young William French from nearby Dummerston, who was inside, died of gunshot wounds at once. Many others were injured, including Daniel Houghton, who died of wounds a week later. Their tombstones are still to be seen in the Westminster cemetery.

Those who could not escape were dragged into the jail, which was in the same building, and locked up. Those who could escape jumped out of windows and ran through the town shouting, "Help, help, they're murdering us!"

Windows flew open and people screamed and ran into the streets. Soon swift runners and horses with furious riders were beating the roads in every direction to spread the news to neighboring towns. By daybreak enraged farmers began racing into town, and by noon four hundred angry citizens were ready for a fight. The first thing they did was to get the prisoners out of jail and hurl the hated sheriff and his followers into the cell instead. Judge Chandler, who was in no way to blame, tried to open the court, but it soon adjourned. This was the last time a New York court met in the Grants.

Two days later, a group of Green Mountain Boys came prancing into town to help, and soon Ethan Allen, who had missed the fight that the local people termed a "massacre," hurried over from Bennington to see what he could do. Ethan had long hoped that the east and west sides of the Grants would unite, and now it had happened!

Somebody suggested that they hold a convention the following month to talk over their problems and make plans. Everybody thought this was a good idea and went home to report what had happened and to elect delegates to the meeting.

When the delegates met in Westminster on April 11, 1775, it was decided that they would fight the government of New York, and they sent a petition to the King asking that they not be considered a part of New York.

While most of the people were happy about the decision of the east and west to work together against New York, some people a few miles to the south in Guilford said they preferred the government of New York, causing much bitterness in town. But the majority of people seemed to agree that the New York government in the Grants must stop.

"We ought to form a new government of our own," said some of the delegates as they stood outside the meeting house in their leather breeches and homespun coats, talking earnestly of politics and government matters.

A week later another group of farmers over in Concord and Lexington, Massachusetts, had a shooting battle with British troops. The Grants' break with New York and the break with England went hand in hand, and finally became one cause in the minds of most of the Grants people.

3. Ticonderoga

LAKE CHAMPLAIN

N.Y.

VT.

FORT
TICONDEROGA

LAKE GEORGE

Ethan's Idea

When Ethan Allen heard about the skirmishes at Lexington and Concord, he was so excited that he decided to act on his own for the cause of liberty.

He and his friends and brothers now owned an interest in a great deal of property on the shores of Lake Champlain, so he knew the area well. He also knew that the British had guns and ammunition and soldiers at Fort Ticonderoga just across the lake. First called Fort Carillon, it had been built by the French and then captured by the British in the French and Indian wars. Why shouldn't the Green Mountain Boys seize the fort so it couldn't be used against the Grants people? He sent word for the Green Mountain Boys to meet him in Castleton on May 9, 1775.

A week before the meeting, some of the Green Mountain Boys gathered at the Catamount Tavern in Bennington to make plans.

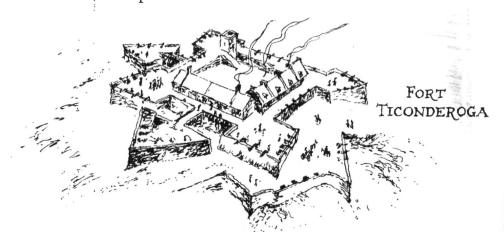

FORT
TICONDEROGA

Spy Noah Phelps

"We need to spy out the place," said Ethan.

"I'll go," said Noah Phelps, liking this kind of adventure. "I'll pretend I'm a woodcutter working on my own."

A few days later, shaggy-headed Noah Phelps walked up to the sentry at the fort.

"What do you want?" grumbled the guard.

"I'm a loyal subject of His Majesty King George, and I need my hair cut. Do you have a barber here?"

The sentry was bored. Talking with this woodcutter was a diversion at least. At last he admitted that the fort did have a barber and he let Phelps in.

Spy Noah Phelps looked about and saw that the fort would be easy to capture, and he hurried back to report to Colonel Allen at Castleton on May 9. Guards were placed on the roads that led to the fort, and messengers were sent out to gather up more troops.

Samuel Beach

"Everybody in this area must be alerted," declared Ethan Allen. "We need a fast walker who knows where every farm in the area is."

"I'll go," volunteered Samuel Beach, son of Gershom Beach of Rutland. "I know every homestead this side of the Green Mountains and every path leading to them."

"We'll attack before dawn on May tenth, so there's no time to lose," said Ethan. "We need to warn Rutland, Pittsford, Brandon, Middlebury, Whiting, and Shoreham."

"I can do it," said Beach, and he did. Over hills and streams and rocks and deep valleys he covered sixty miles on foot in twenty-four hours, taking word of Colonel Allen's plan to even the most remote settlers.

"You're needed at Castleton!" he shouted at cabin doors, which were often nothing more than a bear skin to keep out the wind. And then he hurried miles away to the next dwelling to repeat his message.

Benedict Arnold

In the meantime, Benedict Arnold, a Connecticut druggist and bookseller who liked being a soldier, had started a small militia company. Ambitious and eager, he looked at a map.

"Why shouldn't I raise more soldiers and capture Fort Ticonderoga?" he asked himself. He had no idea that Ethan Allen and the Green Mountain Boys were thinking the same thing. Arnold needed money for the expedition, so he got on his horse and hurried over to Boston to try to get support from the Committee of Safety there. The men on the committee were impressed.

"Let's give the fellow some money to raise troops. I think what he says makes sense," they said. "We'll commission him Colonel."

So the new Colonel Arnold bought himself a fancy uniform and set out for Fort Ticonderoga, planning to enlist soldiers on the way. But as he traveled, disturbing rumors reached him: Ethan Allen and the rag-tag bunch of farmers who called themselves the Green Mountain Boys were already gathering for an assault on the fort—without consulting anybody!

He was so mad that he hurried ahead of his troops to Castleton, and there he and Ethan Allen collided. Benedict Arnold rode into the Green Mountain Boys' headquarters,

waving his credentials from the Committee of Safety and determined to put a stop to Ethan's plans.

"I shall take command," he announced to the astonished Green Mountain Boys who were cleaning their guns for the battle.

"You're crazy! We aren't serving under anybody but Ethan Allen," said the men staunchly.

Allen felt a little sorry for pompous Colonel Arnold, and maybe even a little scared, too. After all, Arnold had impressive-looking papers saying he was in charge.

Ethan Allen thought it over. "All right, you can go with us and march by my side, but I'm the commander of these men, who have volunteered to go with me."

"Aye, aye," cried Allen's men while Arnold fumed. By eleven o'clock in the evening of May 9, 1775, two hundred thirty men had moved from Castleton and assembled at Hand's Cove opposite Fort Ticonderoga.

"Where are the boats?" the men asked each other, peering through the darkness.

Ethan Allen was worried too, for there was not even a rowboat on the shore to carry the men across the lake. The scouts he had sent ahead to find boats must have hit trouble!

Finally, when dawn was only a few hours away, there arrived a large, flat-bottomed boat of the type the French called a "bateau," with a small rowboat behind it. In all, the boats carried only eighty-three men across the water for the attack on the fort.

Nathan Beeman

Once ashore near the fort, in spite of his confident manner Ethan was even more worried. He had never been inside the fort, and even with Noah Phelps's report he needed a guide for the dark approach. Muffled voices broke the pre-dawn silence.

"Colonel Allen, there's a boy here who says he's got to see you," reported one of the soldiers. "I told him he was still wet behind the ears and to go home to his mother, but he's a lad for an argument. He says he knows the fort inside and out, and all he needs is a gun and he can fight as handily as the rest."

"Send me that boy!" ordered Ethan Allen so sharply that the soldier jumped.

The boy, Nathan Beeman, lived on a nearby farm.

"So you want to see Colonel Allen, eh? And you know the fort inside and out?" demanded Ethan.

"Ye-yes, sir," stammered the boy.

"Then how would you like to show us the way in? Can you do it in the dark?" asked Ethan Allen.

Nathan nodded dumbly.

"Then go ask your father quickly if you can go in with us. I don't like enlisting children without a father's leave," said Colonel Allen.

Victory!

When first light was coming over the horizon, Colonel Ethan Allen and Colonel Benedict Arnold in their splendid uniforms, and long-legged and ragged Nathan Beeman climbed the heights to the sally port at Fort Ticonderoga, and the Green Mountain Boys rushed yelling behind them into the sleeping fort. Not a shot was fired; even the sentry's gun failed to go off.

Ethan Allen wrote later that the British commander, Cap-

tain William Delaplace, was standing at the head of the stairs with his pants in his hand as Ethan shouted to him to surrender.

"In whose name?" asked the astonished commander.

"In the name of the great Jehovah and the Continental Congress!" cried Ethan in words that still ring down the years.

More Success—and a Failure

And so it was done, with not a drop of blood shed. Tall and reliable Seth Warner was sent down the lake to capture Crown Point so that Lake Champlain would be safe for the Americans—for the time being. And all the next day most of the Green Mountain Boys rollicked and celebrated by rolling out the kegs of rum and food. They had taken more than sixty prisoners and an enormous lot of cannons and ammunition. There were about forty women and children in the fort, and all of them were well treated and joined in the festivity, it was said.

Benedict Arnold, who was disgusted at the unmilitary activities, was given a chance to show his importance. At last some troops arrived to serve under him, and, with a ship now available, Arnold and his men set off down the lake to capture a British vessel at Fort St. Johns. Arnold not only captured the seventy-ton sloop "Maria" but nine bateaux as well.

Meanwhile, Ethan Allen was doing a bit of fuming himself. "I'm going, too," he had declared, but his clumsy boats, rowed and sailed by loyal Green Mountain Boys, were very slow—so slow, in fact, that he met the victorious Arnold, who was on his way back to Crown Point.

Not very wisely, Ethan stubbornly continued ahead. "Even if Benedict Arnold did get there first, I'm going to take Fort St. Johns and occupy it," he said to his officers.

The men were so tired that they fell on the ground to sleep as soon as they reached the shore near the fort. They would move in the morning, said Colonel Allen. They were rudely awakened at dawn by the arrival of British troops from Montreal, and the Green Mountain Boys ran away so fast that they forgot one of their own men, who failed to wake up. The sleepyhead walked all the way back to Fort Ticonderoga, much put out with Ethan Allen, the hero of Ticonderoga.

4. The New Hampshire Grants Become Vermont

Seth Warner, the New Leader

In June of 1775 Ethan Allen and Seth Warner rode their horses all the way to Philadelphia to tell the Continental Congress that the Green Mountain Boys had taken Fort Ticonderoga, and to urge an invasion of Canada. The men in Congress clapped Ethan and Seth on the back and were so pleased that they recommended that New York pay the costs of the capture, since Ticonderoga was in New York. After all, none of the men had been paid, not even for gunpowder used to fire their rifles, although some money had been raised by Connecticut citizens to help the expedition.

Then things happened in a hurry. Ethan and Seth went to New York City and visited the New York Assembly to discuss the pay for the Green Mountain Boys. Privately they shouted with laughter at this change from being on New York's "wanted" list of the year before, but they agreed that everybody had to pull together now. The New Yorkers were most polite to the gentlemen from the Grants, because they needed the help of the Green Mountain Boys.

"Canada is loyal to England," the men in the Assembly

reasoned. "The British are surely going to put ships on the lake and do who-knows-what to all of us. They might even stir up the Indians!"

New York not only agreed to pay the Green Mountain Boys but also agreed to buy cloth to make each of the five hundred troops a green coat with red facings, and to supply tents and ammunition. From now on the Green Mountain Boys could choose their own officers except for their General, and they would be the "northern department," a major part of the Continental Army commanded by General Philip Schuyler of New York who got his orders from General George Washington, the Commander-in-Chief. Ethan Allen and his men were delighted.

All that was left to be done was to elect their officers, for even the army in the Grants was run on a democratic basis. Not for one minute did Ethan Allen doubt that he would be chosen Colonel of the regiment. A convention was called to meet in Dorset on July 26, 1775. Ethan Allen stirred about, making plans for a grand invasion of Canada he hoped to lead.

But when the men assembled to make their choice of leaders, Seth Warner was elected Colonel. Poor Ethan Allen—he wasn't chosen for a single office, although in addition the men picked Samuel Safford for Major, as well as seven captains and fourteen lieutenants, which included three of Ethan's brothers.

Ethan Allen could have stamped his foot and smashed his sword on the floor in a rage and marched out cursing the people for ingratitude, but he didn't. He was a good sport and took his humiliating defeat better than most men would have done.

"Very well," he said. "If I can't be one of your officers I will give my services as a scout."

The Green Mountain Boys felt that old Ethan was a good fellow, but his military judgment was not as good as that of Seth Warner or some of the other younger men. And Ethan himself turned his wonderful gift of enthusiasm to being a special scout for the Canadian expedition that was beginning to take shape.

Fighting in Canada

At first General Schuyler was in charge, but he was getting old and his big toes hurt with gout, so later in the summer General Richard Montgomery, who had been with General James Wolfe when Quebec was taken from the French in 1759, was put in charge.

Meanwhile Ethan Allen had gone on to Canada to try to persuade Canadians to join the American side. He convinced quite a few, some of whom joined General Montgomery at St. Johns. But Ethan was worried. Things weren't moving fast enough. He knew that winter was coming, and if the Americans didn't strike soon they would lose.

In September he was out scouting, as usual right under the nose of the British General, Sir Guy Carleton, when he ran into a fellow scout, Major John Brown. Ethan's self-confidence had come back with his success in recruiting. Both he and Brown had a number of Canadian troops ready to fight, but still the Americans didn't move forward.

Today historians don't know exactly what happened when Allen and Brown sat down to talk things over. In later years both gave different stories, but we know that Ethan says he came away from the meeting believing that Brown would cross the broad St. Lawrence River with his men and meet Allen and his party just before daybreak outside Montreal. As a signal, they would cry "Huzzah" three times, and then they would rush in together and seize the city before the inhabitants could wake up.

With one hundred ten men, poorly armed and not well trained, Ethan crossed the St. Lawrence River north of Montreal during the night. At daybreak, he wrote later, he waited for Brown's signal, which never came. And it was too late to try to retreat.

Montreal was on an island. There was nothing to do but try to fight it out with the British, who soon discovered the invading band. Allen's men were quickly defeated and Ethan Allen, alas, was taken prisoner and put aboard the warship *Gaspée,* where he was locked in irons, to be taken to prison in England. It was the spring of 1778—two and a half years later—before he was exchanged and returned to America. What happened to Major Brown and his troops on that September night at Montreal was never explained, but history says that he was a brave and good man.

In a few weeks Seth Warner and some of the Green Mountain Boys stopped British General Carleton when he set out toward Lake Champlain to take aid to the British fort at St. Johns. This was a turning point, for soon General Montgomery and the American forces took Montreal. In November many of the Green Mountain Boys were honorably discharged until the weather warmed up.

In the meantime, Benedict Arnold tried to invade Canada from another direction. Almost freezing to death, he and his men traveled up the Kennebec River and through the Maine wilderness to Canada. On December 31, 1775, they all joined forces under General Montgomery and tried to capture Quebec City, but they failed. General Montgomery was killed, Colonel Arnold was badly wounded, and General David Wooster of New York was put in command.

"I need the Green Mountain Boys back again," he said. And in March, Seth Warner took troops through nasty late-winter weather to answer the call.

When British reinforcements arrived in Canada in May of 1776 the half-starved Americans retreated, many dying of smallpox on the march. Down in the Grants the people were terrified for fear that the British would attack. Rumors flew that the Indians were being stirred up, and people were warned to move back to Connecticut or Massachusetts.

But most settlers who had worked hard beyond belief for their stakes in the wilderness set their jaws and declared, "We'll stay, thank you!" And even when fathers went off to war, as most of them did, the women and children took over, stubbornly holding on to their hard-won acres.

Fort Independence

In July of 1776 it took a week, more or less, to get news from Philadelphia to the Grants, because reports were carried by travelers who came on foot or on horseback. When the Declaration of Independence was signed on the Fourth of July, the Green Mountain Boys and other American troops were guarding a rocky point that sticks out into Lake Champlain opposite Fort Ticonderoga, and on July 28, 1776, soldiers were working as hard as they could to complete a new fort there.

"Never seen such heavy rocks," grumbled a soldier as he and his comrade struggled to heave a great boulder into place to make a wall.

"These walls might save our lives, if the heat doesn't kill

us first," puffed the other. "Hark, I hear the call to come on
the run to the parade grounds!"

"Ten-*shun!*" shouted the sergeant when the troops assembled. Quiet fell as Colonel Arthur St. Clair, message in hand,
stood before them.

"Down in Philadelphia," he announced, "a Declaration of
Independence has been signed by the Continental Congress.
The representatives have broken their ties with England and
pledged us to fight for independence!"

Not being a colony like the rest, the Grants had no representative in Philadelphia although the Green Mountain Boys
had been fighting for this independence for fourteen months.
Nevertheless, they cheered and danced about in high spirits.

The sergeant shouted for silence and Colonel St. Clair
continued, "From now on this new fort will be called Fort
Independence."

There were more shouts and huzzahs from the soldiers.
Now they felt that they officially had a country to fight for.
They went back to their back-breaking work with zeal.

Today the rock foundations of this fort can still be seen by
hikers who climb the rough trail to Mount Independence in
the town of Orwell.

Conventions and Government

All over the Grants, people were busy. Jacob Bayley was
building a military road from Newbury, on the Connecticut
River, north to Westfield, near the present Canadian border.
Bayley didn't like Ethan Allen and his friends, but they all
favored the cause of liberty and worked together.

In the meantime, citizens had been holding conventions to
try to work out some form of government. They had had no

courts and no laws since they had cut themselves off from New York, and thoughtful men were concerned, knowing that lawful leaders must be elected and a government established. In January of 1776 there was a meeting at the house of Mr. Cephas Kent in Dorset, where delegates from eighteen towns met and chose a committee to prepare a letter to take to the Continental Congress, telling of the problems they had with New York.

Captain Heman Allen, Ethan's brother, met with a convention of delegates and reported on his trip to Philadelphia, where the Congress had not been favorable to the Grants' side in the quarrel with New York.

"We'll form our own association!" shouted someone.

"Down with New York!" cried another.

"Let's fight!" came another voice.

They were acting like disorderly school children in their excitement. Captain Joseph Bowker, the chairman, pounded for order. People were so eager to be heard that the very first item of business was: "Voted: First. That not more than one person be allowed to speak at the same time, and only by leave of the chairman."

Then Heman Allen was heard. "Although the Continental Congress did not support us, we have friends in Philadelphia. Many a man hinted that we should declare ourselves an independent state," he told them.

On July 25, 1776, forty-nine people adopted an "association," or a pact, in which they pledged to support each other in their cause. Here is part of what they wrote and signed, with the spelling and punctuation of the day:

"We, the Subscribers, inhabitants of the District of Land, commonly called and known by the name of the New Hampshire Grants, do Voluntarily and Solemnly Engage under all the ties held sacred amongst Mankind, at the

Risque of our Lives and fortunes, to Defend, by Arms, the United American States, against the Hostile Attempts of the British Fleets and Armies, until the present unhappy Controversy between the two Countries shall be Settled."

It was decided that delegates should get as many signatures as possible in their own towns. Nobody would ask the women to sign, because in those days only men could vote, but boys of sixteen could put their mark or name to the association. In September the delegates met again to talk about becoming a state. Not everybody wanted to fight Britain, but the voices of the Loyalists were drowned out by those who did.

"Go home again and find out if the people want to become a state," the convention leaders told the delegates. "We'll meet again in October at Westminster."

The Battle of Valcour

When October came, many of the men in the Grants had grabbed their muskets and gone to Fort Ticonderoga and Fort Independence to help protect their land from a British invasion force that was sailing up Lake Champlain.

During the summer, while the people in the Grants were getting signatures in support of statehood, Benedict Arnold was promoted to Brigadier General, and was put in charge of building ships of war for the Americans. The clever Arnold sent to New England seaports and got experienced carpenters and necessary equipment, and set up a shipyard at Fort Ticonderoga. He worked like a demon to get the fleet built, for he knew that the British were building ships too, and that there would soon be a fight for control of Lake Champlain.

On August 24, Arnold set out in command of his fleet of three schooners, two sloops, three galleys, and eight gondolas, and was hit almost at once by a dreadful storm. But the ships were sturdy and they rode it out, and by September they were at Windmill Point, only five miles from the British fleet.

Arnold made his stand at Valcour Island near South Hero, and the battle began on October 11. The British had seventy vessels with ninety-three guns and seven hundred seamen, and, because they were sure that the American ships were bottled up, they withdrew when night came. But they were wrong: Arnold slipped his spunky little navy so quietly through the British lines in the darkness that nobody heard them.

When the British found that the Americans had outwitted them, they set out in pursuit. Arnold, realizing that the much superior force would overcome his fleet, ran his ships aground near the mouth of Otter Creek and ordered his men to get to shore.

"General Arnold was the last man to leave," said the sailors admiringly as they walked back to Fort Ticonderoga. "He's a brave one, all right. I feared he might be burned alive."

Arnold had set fire to the ships rather than let them be captured, and was the last man to jump into the water from his blazing flapship. Only one American ship fell into British hands, and none of his men was killed.

The plans of General Sir Guy Carleton had been greatly delayed by Arnold. The British commander thought about the thirteen thousand troops assembled at the forts to oppose him, and realized that winter would soon be coming to freeze the lake. Rather than risk getting caught in the ice he turned around and went back to Canada.

The Americans shouted with joy because they were safe until spring, at least, and Arnold was everybody's hero. Arnold thought he should have been promoted for his bravery, but some higher officers were jealous of him and prevented it. Arnold became so bitter that he later joined the British side, but he deserves to be remembered for his skill and bravery at the Battle of Valcour.

The Vote for Independence at Westminster

On January 15, 1777, town representatives gathered at Westminster for an historic convention, which lasted three days. The delegates had had plenty of time to talk with their neighbors to find out how they felt about becoming an independent state. Throughout the fall and early winter, men had sat by cabin fireplaces warming themselves, sipping mugs of cider, and talking politics while the women and children listened.

On January 16, 1777, at eight o'clock in the morning it was still dark enough to have candles lit on the chairman's desk, but the meeting opened. Before the day was over, a committee was chosen to write a declaration of independence that would make "the New Hampshire Grants a new and separate state."

"I think we should call ourselves 'New Connecticut,'" said one. "Most of us came here from Connecticut."

"Too long a name," argued another. "Besides, some of us came from Massachusetts."

But the name New Connecticut was agreed upon, and on the 17th of January the actual declaration of independence of the little state in the Green Mountains was voted on, and approved. A committee was chosen to go to Philadelphia to tell the Continental Congress that they wanted to join the United States.

When New York heard about New Connecticut some of the Yorkers got indignant. "Why, those rascals can't be independent," some of them declared. "New Connecticut indeed! We'll put a stop to that."

So the New York delegates at the Continental Congress told the other members not to listen to those upstarts from the New Hampshire Grants who were using the war as an opportunity to cut themselves off from New York. Other states were worried that parts of their territories might follow the Grants' example.

The Congress was in an uncomfortable spot. New York was powerful, yet the men from New Connecticut seemed to have a good cause, too. The Congress hemmed and hawed and finally did nothing at all, in order to keep New York happy.

But the committee from Westminster did a lot of talking and won some friends. Dr. Jonas Fay, Colonel Thomas Chittenden, Dr. Reuben Jones, Colonel Jacob Bayley, and Captain Heman Allen were stout-hearted men who soon found an ally in an old friend of Ethan Allen's, Dr. Thomas Young of Philadelphia. Dr. Young invited them to his house and gave them sympathetic and intelligent advice.

Vermont Gets a Name

"Do you have a constitution for New Connecticut?" asked Dr. Young.

"No," admitted the men. "That will take time."

"You can't have a state without a constitution," said Dr. Young.

THE GRANTS BECOME VERMONT/68

Dr. Young slapped his knee in excitement. "I think I have the answer for you," he said. He drew from his desk some legal-looking papers. "This is the Constitution of Pennsylvania," he said, laying the document on the table for the men to see. "It is the most liberal and best constitution yet written. Why, it's the work of Dr. Benjamin Franklin himself, and of Thomas Paine, that great friend of liberty. What better model could you have? Make a change here and there to suit your local situations."

New
Connecticut

The committee from the Grants read over the document eagerly, exclaiming excitedly as they read. With a few changes, this constitution would fit New Connecticut's needs and be a firm foundation for the future government, they agreed.

"As for your name," said Dr. Young as the men finished their enthusiastic reading, "there's already an area in Pennsylvania called New Connecticut. Would you not think another name would suit you better?"

"We've tried to find a better name," admitted the men. "New Connecticut was just the best of some bad suggestions, perhaps. Have you something in mind?"

"I have," said Dr. Young triumphantly. "Indeed I have. I have a name that will tell about your Green Mountains, which hold you together; a name that suggests the early French settlements, which would be pleasing to the French, who we hope will soon be our allies against the British."

"Tell us, tell us," murmured the men.

" 'Verd Mont,' meaning 'green mountain' in the French language. It would be more original and slip more easily off the tongue if you called it 'Ver-mont.' "

"Vermont," said the men, testing the word. "Vermont. Vermont it shall be!" cried Colonel Chittenden. "We will take it back to our people, and I'll wager that they will

VERD MONT

VERMONT

choose both the name and the constitution."

Colonel Chittenden was right. When they got back home in time for the convention in June of 1777 in Windsor the name Vermont was unanimously adopted by the seventy-two delegates. It was decided to have a constitutional convention in July, and on June 23 the towns voted for delegates to it.

Throughout the colonies, the people were thinking of military matters in June of 1777. British General John Burgoyne with a mighty army was moving south toward Fort Ticonderoga. A proclamation was read to observe June 18 as a day of prayer and fasting. The infant Vermont was facing a troubled world.

Burgoyne

The name of "Gentleman Johnny" Burgoyne, as people called him, was on everybody's tongue, and he was moving up Lake Champlain from Canada with what one observer called "the most splendid regatta you can possibly conceive." He had seven thousand troops ready to attack the American people who had rebelled and declared their independence.

What was worse, he had stirred up the Indians and sent a proclamation to the Vermonters along Lake Champlain and to the people south of the lake around Hubbardton, Rutland, and Pawlet warning them to turn themselves in to the British or be captured and killed.

"I have but to give stretch to the Indian forces under my direction, and they amount to thousands," proclaimed Burgoyne, "to overtake the enemies of Great Britain and America."

Vermonters quaked in their boots, but once again most of them decided that their land was too dear to them to leave, even when faced with the news that Burgoyne had promised bounty for white scalps from the five hundred Iroquois troops under his command.

On unlucky Friday the thirteenth of June, 1777, General St. Clair was assigned to take over the few American troops at Fort Independence and Fort Ticonderoga. It was too late to organize defenses and there weren't enough soldiers—only three thousand in all, and many of them were sick. St. Clair looked at the steep hill next to Fort Ticonderoga.

"The British can never take that," he said to his officers who had suggested fortifying it. "It's too steep to get all the artillery to the top."

Imagine his surprise to wake up a few mornings later to find the British all settled in on the mountain, which they had named Mount Defiance, with their guns in place overlooking both the American forts. There was nothing for the Americans to do but get out as fast as possible. Some got away by boat to Skenesboro, where Burgoyne caught them; the rest thought they could escape by land.

Fort Independence and Fort Ticonderoga were connected by a floating bridge across the narrow strip of water that separated them. Early in the morning of July 6 the troops from Fort Ticonderoga crept over the bridge and joined the troops at Fort Independence. Then they all tiptoed down the

heights and began to retreat toward Castleton so quietly that the British would never have seen them except that someone carelessly set fire to a building.

"After them! After them! Catch them! The Americans are escaping!" shouted the British sentries, alerted by the flames at four o'clock in the morning.

The last of the Americans were just clearing the fort when the British set out to chase the retreating troops.

Colonel Seth Warner had stopped at Hubbardton to rest and wait for stragglers, and it was here at about dawn of July 7, 1777, that British troops overtook and attacked them in the Battle of Hubbardton. Warner's men were doing very well until some hired German troops arrived to help the British, and the Vermont troops took to the woods.

The fighting at Hubbardton, the only battle of the Revolution to take place on the soil of present-day Vermont, was over.

Vermont Gets a Constitution

While all this fighting was going on, the convention to draft a Constitution for the new state was meeting at Windsor. There was a nervous excitement among the thirty-four delegates, for they knew that Burgoyne was approaching. On July 8, 1777, the weather was sticky hot. The exhausted men wiped their foreheads as they sat in the stifling room, framing the Constitution which they hoped to adopt for Vermont.

Most of the work was done. The Constitution began by telling why Vermont had separated from New York, and then listed a declaration of rights of the citizens, including freedom of speech, freedom to worship, freedom of assembly, and justice in the courts.

"We'll have no slaves in Vermont," said one delegate. "Let's put that in our Bill of Rights."

"Aye, aye," agreed the others, and Vermont became the first state to forbid slavery in its constitution.

Every man over twenty-one years old who had lived in Vermont for a year could vote and hold office, whether or not he owned property. "Poor people have a right to take part in the government, too," they decided. This was the first time any state had put such a provision in its constitution.

"Private property ought to be subservient to public uses when necessity requires it . . ." said the Constitution. "That's right," said the delegates. "A man's property can't be used only to please himself. The public has some rights over all the land."

And so they worked on into the afternoon.

There was a clatter of horse's hoofs in the courtyard.

"Hold my horse, lad," cried the rider to a boy who was lurking by the open door, hoping to hear what was going on inside. The boy caught the reins as the messenger dashed into the building just as a violent thunderclap shook the heavens.

"Our forces have evacuated Fort Ticonderoga and Fort Independence!" the newcomer shouted. "There's fighting at Hubbardton. Every man is needed!"

Delegates leaped to their feet, tipping over chairs and throwing down their papers.

"If Fort Ticonderoga and Fort Independence are lost, then there's no protection left," someone shouted.

The men looked at each other in alarm and headed for the door amid cries of dismay.

"Gentlemen!" called the chairman, Colonel Joseph Bowker, as he rapped for order. "Torrents of rain are beginning to fall. We cannot leave in such a storm. Let us finish our work on the Constitution and then leave." He knew that with events as they were, the delegates might never get together again to agree on a Constitution, which was essential if Vermont was to survive politically.

And so they did. Quickly the delegates consented to the last points, approved the document unanimously, and even remembered that they must choose a twelve-man Council of Safety to govern Vermont until elections could be held by the people.

The rain stopped, the newly adopted Constitution was turned over to Ira Allen to be printed for the people to see, and the men set out as fast as their horses and feet could carry them to help fight the enemy and protect their families and farms.

The new State of Vermont was born at war, and no birth ever needed a fairy godmother more than this one did.

From the title page of Vermont's first Constitution

5. The Republic
of Vermont

IRA ALLEN

Ira Saves the Day

As soon as the twelve men who had been chosen for the governing council saw that their families were safe, they met in Manchester on July 11, 1777, and elected Thomas Chittenden president of the Council of Safety, and Ira Allen the secretary.

The Council had problems aplenty. For one, the mighty army of Burgoyne was moving closer, but the frail new state had no troops of its own, and it was agreed to ask New Hampshire and Connecticut and Massachusetts to send men to help fight the battle that was sure to come. For another, the Council had to be on guard against the American Tories who were loyal to England—some of whom had even banded together into a brigade called the Queen's Loyal Rangers, to fight fellow Vermonters. And on top of these worries, refugees were pouring into the town ahead of the British force, and the Council had no money to help support them, or to pay for an army if it had one.

The newly elected president put his head in his hands

and thought hard. He was a generous patriot though not a rich one.

"I'll give what I have," he said. "I have ten head of cattle that'll be worth something."

"What will your wife think of that?" asked someone.

"She approves. She even told me that she would give her gold necklace to a state treasury," replied Mr. Chittenden.

And then the others got up and pledged what they had, for they believed in Vermont. Some offered to raise troops and pay them, while others offered goods. Nobody had much money.

"Even if all of us give all we can there's still not enough to raise the kind of army we need," argued Ira Allen, who was twenty-one years old and by far the youngest person there. "We must have a whole regiment and we must pay them properly."

The Council laughed at the impractical young fellow.

"I move that Ira Allen come up with a plan to raise enough money to pay for as many troops as we need and to have the answer ready by tomorrow morning when we meet again," cried Nathan Clark, half in fun, half in hopes that Ira, who certainly was smart, might think up some scheme.

"Hear, hear!" cried the others, and the meeting adjourned with laughter and a few slaps on the back for the slender young man. Ira Allen went back to his room and thought and thought. About midnight an idea so good struck him that he burst out laughing, and when the Council met at sunrise Ira took the floor, hardly able to hide his high spirits.

"Gentlemen, I have found the solution to our money problems," he announced with a broad smile.

The others looked at each other in amazement. Impossible!

"We'll seize the loyalist Tories' property and sell it or rent it and use the money for the treasury," said Ira triumphantly.

There was a moment of silence.

"It'll work, by Jove!" cried one member.

"Huzzah for Ira!"

"We'll do it!" were the shouts. The Council adopted the plan at once, and in a few days they moved the headquarters to Bennington.

The Battle of Bennington

Over in New Hampshire, General John Stark heard that help was needed at Bennington. He sent a message that they could count on him to bring some New Hampshire troops, but he wasn't taking orders from anybody in the Continental Army, as the American forces were called. From New York, General Schuyler sent gunpowder, but he was concentrating on preparing to fight the main force of Burgoyne, who commanded Brunswick and Hessian mercenaries—soldiers from Germany who hired out to fight for any side that would pay them—and Tory brigades, and Indian recruits.

"General Burgoyne wants to steal our supplies that are stored in Bennington," spies reported. Everybody knew by now that Burgoyne's plan was to move south and meet other British troops that were expected to move north, and in that way cut off Vermont and the rest of New England and make the American army surrender.

And Vermonters, proud of their new name, gritted their teeth and said, "Johnny Burgoyne, we're going to lick you!"

General Stark and his New Hampshire troops hurried to Bennington. When they heard that the enemy was moving closer, they got ready for a battle about eight miles west of town, in what is now Hoosick, New York.

At three o'clock in the afternoon of August 16, 1777, troops under Stark and Warner attacked the British, who surrendered after two hours of hot fighting. The prisoners were collected and were being marched to Bennington when more British troops arrived to start a second battle.

General Stark turned to his men with fire in his eye.

"Men, there are the redcoats. Before night they are ours, or Molly Stark will be a widow."

"Molly" was the nickname for the General's wife, and so famous did the saying become that today the Molly Stark Highway crosses southern Vermont to Bennington, where a tall monument to the Battle of Bennington overlooks the town.

The Americans won the second battle that afternoon, with many British troops routed and retreating, and the rest surrendering about dark. There were many dead and wounded on both sides, and the rejoicing over victory was mixed with sadness in Bennington as the battle casualties were brought in. One of the dead was John Fay, son of the landlord of the Catamount Tavern, and there was hardly a family there who did not lose a relative.

"Where can we put all these prisoners?" the Council members asked each other.

"I guess we'll have to use the meeting house for the jail and ask the people of the town to take in the wounded," they decided. "The women will care for them."

The women who nursed men from both sides were Vermont's first volunteer nurses. Tradition says that the nurses cared for the sick soldiers for several months in a crude hospital built by the town.

To feed the prisoners, the Council borrowed huge iron potash kettles to cook masses of cornmeal mush. As soon as possible they marched the prisoners to Boston. The Bennington people treated the enemy troops decently, but the story goes that the women of the town were so angry at the American Tories who fought against their own people that the women marched them through the streets tied with "bed ropes" from their family beds. In those days beds had ropes, forming a sort of hammock, instead of springs.

After the battle, the Vermont soldiers carried away the captured cannons to use in later fighting. Today some of these big guns sit in front of the State House in Montpelier.

Because of the victory at Bennington, Burgoyne and his entire army were defeated at nearby Saratoga, New York, on October 17, 1777, the turning point of the Revolution. Now Vermont could turn her attention to her government.

Vermont's First Elections and Assembly

Gov. Thomas
Chittenden

The people chose Thomas Chittenden as their governor when elections were held in March of 1778. He had a council of twelve to help him, and the elected representatives from the towns formed an Assembly. Judges were elected by the Assembly, so now there were executive, judiciary, and legislative branches of the government of the new state. They adopted the laws of Connecticut to use until they could develop their own.

"What are we going to do about the Tories and their land?" was probably one of the first questions the men asked each other as they gathered for the first Assembly meeting at Windsor on March 12, 1778.

"We'll have to set up a special court for taking the Tory land," said someone else. About two hundred Tories had land taken from them, and many went to Canada where the

British government gave them new lands in reward for their loyalty to England.

Tearful children said goodbye to their playmates, not understanding why their neighbors had to move away. Tories who changed their minds took an oath of allegiance and were welcomed home.

There were other problems too, and the most troublesome of all was the matter of sixteen New Hampshire towns along the Connecticut River who looked across at their neighbors and decided they wanted to become part of Vermont. The Assembly decided that it could not say "no" to old friends, and the majority voted to admit them, stirring up the greatest tempest yet.

"Those loonies who call the Grants the state of Vermont think they'll annex part of New Hampshire, eh?" said the New Hampshire leaders in amazement. "We'll stop that!"

Border Problems

New York was doing her best to convince the Congress that Vermont should not be recognized as a state, and Canada remained a bitter enemy on the north. The British controlled Lake Champlain from which they attacked Middlebury and captured some townspeople. Vermont could not afford to get in a quarrel with New Hampshire at this point, so the Assembly changed its mind and told the New Hampshire towns that they could not join Vermont after all.

What a squabble! The New Hampshire towns were mad, and their friends in Vermont were so angry at their own Vermont government that some towns in the Green Mountain State said they might pull out and join New Hampshire, or form an independent state along the Connecticut River

Valley, which made the Vermont Assembly change its mind again. In February of 1779, things got even worse for the new state when Massachusetts laid a claim to Vermont, too.

These conflicting claims were so confusing that the Congress said that New York, New Hampshire, and Massachusetts should allow Congress to settle Vermont's boundary problems, without so much as mentioning Vermont's feelings on the matter.

"New Hampshire and New York are going to split Vermont down the middle of the Green Mountains," ran the rumor.

Vermont farmers clung angrily to their land. "I'd like to see some of them try splitting up our state," said men defiantly.

Back and forth the fight went for several years. By July of 1781 some New York towns decided that they, too, would like to become part of Vermont, which would have then become a state of one hundred two towns stretching from the Hudson River to east of the Connecticut River.

With the Revolutionary War almost at an end, New York decided to send troops to fight it out with Vermont.

"New York is massing troops, and they say they are coming over to tear Vermont apart," gasped the messenger who brought the news to Governor Chittenden and his Council.

"Then we'll fight back!" said the men on the Council. "Ethan's back. He'll lead us." Vermont and New York soldiers glared at each other for a week across the border, but nobody shot his gun.

And then George Washington turned his attention to the problem. He wrote to Governor Chittenden and told him that if Vermont would stop playing with her boundaries and return the towns to New York and New Hampshire, so Vermont's limits would be back where the Grants' boundaries had been at the beginning of the Revolution, he would try to

persuade the Congress to recognize Vermont as the Fourteenth State.

The Assembly returned the land and sent agents down to
Philadelphia in good faith to arrange for Vermont to join the
United States, but the Congress refused to accept Vermont.

"We'll go it alone, then," Vermont declared. "We became
an independent country in 1777, and we'll stay independent."

And she remained a little republic outside the government
of the United States until 1791. There are many stories of
Vermont's stormy existence during the fourteen years between her birth at Windsor and her joining the Union as the
Fourteenth State.

The Return of Ethan Allen

In 1778, not long after Vermont was established, Ethan Allen,
who had been a British prisoner since 1775, was exchanged
and returned home. He had missed the exciting years of
Vermont's declaring her independence, but he was more
than ready to serve her again.

As soon as he got home things began to happen, as they
always seemed to do when Ethan was around. One day word
was received that the two small daughters of a neighbor
were lost in the woods. People stopped what they were
doing and turned out to hunt for the lost children, but by the
end of the third day hope was lost.

"We'll never find them. What chance have little girls
against wolves, rushing rivers, and cold nights?" asked one
of the neighbors. The sorrowful parents bowed their heads
and accepted the dreadful verdict as the searchers gave up
and headed for home.

"I don't believe they're dead," said Ethan, always optimistic. "I'm sticking with the hunt if I have to do it alone." Then he jumped on a stump and urged the others to stay on, pleading so hard that tears rolled down his cheeks. So the hunt continued, with every man back in the forest. A few hours later they found the children, sobbing and starving, at the foot of a giant tree.

A few days later Ethan went to Bennington because the Assembly was meeting there, and he was certain to see many of his old friends. The town was in an uproar, for there was going to be a public hanging, something that had never happened before in the Grants. David Redding, a Tory who was accused of stealing cattle and ammunition, had been convicted by a jury of six men, but Vermont's first lawyer, John Burnham, had arrived just in time to tell them that they should have a jury of twelve.

So the hanging was postponed, and the people who had come from far away to watch were so disappointed that they threatened to steal the prisoner and lynch him!

Ethan Allen, who was appointed to prosecute the case, jumped on a stump, his favorite place for making speeches, and in his booming voice demanded that the people go home and come back next week.

"I will guarantee you a hanging if I have to be strung up myself," he cried, and the idea was so ridiculous that the people laughed and went away in a good humor.

David Redding was convicted by a jury of twelve and hanged, but the Bennington people were uneasy about it. There were stories whispered that the ghost of David Redding walked, for he should have been tried by a military court. Later the Assembly was so ashamed of the affair that all the records were destroyed. Instead of being buried, David Redding's bones were used by doctors for study, but people believed they brought bad luck. Today they are in a museum, still unburied.

The Haldimand Plot

One day in May of 1780, when the border problems were worrying independent Vermont, Ethan Allen was walking down the street in Arlington, where he now lived, when a stranger handed him a letter, and then disappeared. When Ethan opened the mysterious letter he found it was from a Tory, Beverly Robinson, who wanted Ethan to tell him if Vermont would like to be a separate colony directly under the British Crown. Ethan showed the letter to his brother Ira and to Governor Chittenden. The three of them studied it, wondering what to do.

"It's well known that on the Canadian border there are thousands of British troops waiting to pounce on us at any minute," said one.

"We have no American troops here, and New York wouldn't protect us unless we'd knuckle down to her rule," said another.

"There aren't enough men in Vermont to outlast a real border fight with the British," said the other. "We have only two hundred and thirty men under arms. They have ten times that many, and more."

"They know we have no friendly neighbors to help us now, with all these boundary troubles, and the Congress keeps turning us down," said Governor Chittenden. "Canada knows that we would be tempted by such an offer, yet I am not ready to become a province of Canada."

They continued to debate the matter, and finally decided to keep quiet, not to answer the letter, and to wait and see if the Congress would at last change its mind and invite Vermont to join them.

About a year later another letter came to Ethan asking if Vermont would like to exchange prisoners under a separate truce. This letter was brought by an old friend of Ethan's, Justus Sherwood, a Tory who came under a flag of truce to Colonel Ethan Allen at his camp in Castleton.

"England would welcome Vermont into the British Empire," whispered Sherwood. "You would be wise to listen. Governor Frederick Haldimand sends his greetings."

The soldiers in the camp noticed all this and rumors began to fly.

"Something fishy is going on," said one soldier to another

"Are the government leaders playing with treason?" asked another hotly. Benedict Arnold had just been found guilty of treason, and the thought was in many minds.

Ethan's cousin, Colonel Seth Warner, was very sick and soon would die, but he came to see Ethan.

"Is it true," he demanded accusingly, "that you are planning to sell out to the British?" Ethan didn't answer.

Governor Chittenden and his advisors decided to send both letters to the Congress. Perhaps they would finally be frightened into admitting Vermont to the Union if they knew of Britain's interest. Up on Lake Champlain British ships were waiting for an answer, quite sure that Vermont would choose England.

Ira Allen, now Vermont's first Secretary of State, played a delaying game with the British, writing them secret letters to keep them guessing. Luckily the matter was soon settled for good when the Revolutionary War ended. The disappointed British on Lake Champlain turned around and went back to their posts.

Nobody knows to this day whether or not the leaders

meant to deliver Vermont to the British, or if it was only a scheme to save their state or a lever to force Congress to act. The correspondence, called the Haldimand Papers, can be read in libraries, where people may study them and decide their version of the truth of the matter.

The Story of Zadock Steele

While the new republic that was Vermont was struggling along, in October of 1780 Zadock Steele, a bachelor from Randolph, was getting in his winter wood when he heard the shouts of a neighbor.

"Zadock, Indians and British are burning Royalton! We must all get prepared. They're killing and plundering."

Zadock put down his ax and hurried to help his neighbors move their families and their possessions into a safe spot in the woods. There was a feel of snow in the air as they built the stockade.

"The Indians and British will take the river and when they're done here they'll go to Brookfield," said one grim-faced man. "Someone ought to warn Brookfield."

"I'll go," said Zadock. "I hope the snow holds off."

Weary Zadock Steele set out, and soon it began to snow with such fury that he had to turn back. It was too late to find his neighbors, who were hidden in the woods, so he returned to his own house, hoping the snow had stopped the Indians. He was awakened at dawn by the screeches and shouts of three hundred Indians who had surrounded his house.

Before he was wide awake they had set fire to his house, and he found himself captured and marching to Canada. His clothes were taken away and he was dressed like the Indians,

who assigned him a "mother" and a "brother" from their group.

There were many other prisoners on the long march. Finally he was put in a British prison on an island in the St. Lawrence River. He and some other prisoners dug their way out in a daring escape, and Zadock Steele returned two years later to Randolph. He wrote a book about his adventures called *The Indian Captive: Or, a Narrative of the Captivity & Sufferings of Zadock Steele,* and it still can be found in some libraries.

Yorker Warfare

Not everybody in Vermont wanted to be independent. In the southeastern part of the state, then called Cumberland County, there was a stubborn group that remained loyal to New York, and Vermont had trouble with these Yorkers within its own borders who openly defied the Vermont laws.

The Yorkers held conventions, refused to obey the Vermont officials, and stayed in close touch with their Yorker friends across the border because they thought New York Governor George Clinton would back them up. So they grew more and more bold, and bitterly divided the people in the towns by electing their own officers who were forever fighting the officials elected by the pro-Vermont citizens.

In 1779, Guilford was the largest town in Vermont with a population of three thousand, the majority of whom were pro-Yorker. Many people in Putney, Brattleboro, Marlboro, and Halifax and other towns of the area followed Guilford's lead. One of the best known of the Yorkers was Charles Phelps of Marlboro, a bright and able lawyer who violently

opposed the Vermont government, and kept things stirring to a boiling point.

In 1779, when Ethan Allen had been home for a year, he had a gala party at the Catamount Tavern in Bennington and invited all his friends to come and celebrate the anniversary of his return. At the height of the merriment, while Ethan was booming out stories of his captivity, a dispatch rider arived with a message from Governor Chittenden. An uprising had taken place at Putney and was spreading to Brattleboro, Guilford, and Westminster. Would Ethan take charge of halting the uprising?

One hundred fifty volunteers, mostly Green Mountain Boys, turned out at once, and their number grew as they galloped from one town to another, shouting and beating drums. They arrested thirty-six people, putting them in jail at Westminster, and then turned them loose when most of them took an oath of allegiance to Vermont. In this way Ethan scared some of the faint-hearted into having more respect for the Vermont government.

In 1782, when Ethan was officially the head of the Vermont militia, he was sent out to put a stop to more uprisings. When he and his Green Mountain Boys roared through Guilford, the people did not seem scared at all when Ethan shouted at them in his mighty voice.

Just beyond the town Ethan himself found a reason to be scared. Half of the men of Guilford, hidden in ambush, leaped out and surprised the party, which broke and ran. A bit ashamed, Ethan and his men assembled again. The Guilford people had a good laugh this time, and nobody was hurt.

But that was not the end of the matter. As historian Zadock Thompson wrote:

"During the years of 1783 and 1784, the enmity of the

parties was carried to an alarming extent. Social order was at an end; physicians were not allowed to visit the sick without a pass from the several committees. Handbills from various quarters inflamed the minds of the people. Relatives and neighbors were openly arrayed against each other. The laws of Vermont were disregarded by the partisans of New York, and her executive officers were openly resisted."

Before the "Cumberland War"—or the "Yorker War," as the series of squabbles was sometimes called—was over in 1785, many people had been jailed or banished, some property was confiscated, and two people had been killed in the disturbances. Although New York did not help the Vermont Yorkers with force, Governor Clinton did send a number of letters of complaint about Vermont to Congress and finally agreed to set aside eight square miles in New York State where Yorker sympathizers could settle if they cared to leave Vermont. But most of the people were forgiven and they settled back into life at home under Vermont law.

The End of the Revolution

"Maybe we'll have some peace ourselves now," said war-weary men when the Treaty of Paris formally ended the Revolutionary War in 1783.

"Looks as if Ethan will put a stop to those scrapping Yorkers down Guilford way before long," said another hopefully.

There were no more border fights with the neighboring states, and Canada was causing no problems. Vermont people had even stopped thinking much about joining the United States, for they realized that Vermont had fewer war debts to pay than her neighbors did.

But problems of another sort arose to rock the state. Citizens were angry at the courts, which were trying great numbers of bad-debt cases, for the people had no money to pay private debts or taxes. Mobs stormed the courts in Rutland and Windsor, and the militia was called out.

Arrests for disturbances were common in Vermont in this period just after the end of the Revolutionary War. In 1787 the Vermont legislature passed some laws to help people who had no money by letting them use cattle or grain or other products to pay their debts.

Thomas Chittenden kept on being Governor, getting elected every year except one for Vermont's first nineteen years. They called him "One-eyed Tom" because he had lost the sight of one eye. He never put on airs, and through all the years he was Governor he continued to slop his pigs, serve ale at his tavern, feed the stock, and work in his fields. He had ten children, all of whom lived to grow up, a rare thing in those days.

When the Revolution formally ended, there were thirty thousand people living in Vermont, and more people arrived in the state daily, on sleds or in carts or boats, or on foot over military roads, Indian trails, or along river banks. Families with sturdy children trudging along behind, carrying loads that must have seemed heavy beyond belief, camped at night and traveled by day. It seemed that everybody wanted to come to Vermont.

Elias Smith

Elias Smith was thirteen years old when he left his home in Lyme, Connecticut, and traveled 180 miles on foot with his family to a new home in Woodstock. In April of 1782, wrote Elias Smith, for this is a true story taken from a real diary,

Elias's father and elder brother came to Vermont to set up shelter and clear land, and then returned to Connecticut, full of the glories of Vermont, to get Elias and the rest of the family.

Says Elias: "The thought of going on the journey was peculiarly pleasing to me. . . . Although I was obliged to walk almost the whole way, yet my mind was so gratified in seeing new towns, large villages, elegant buildings, magnificent bridges, lofty mountains and deep valleys."

Finally they got within a mile of the new house site. Elias was weary but excited. What would the new home be like?

"A considerable part of this mile a cart had never been," he writes. "It took us till sometime in the afternoon to cut away the logs and stumps so that the team could pass along. After many sweats and pulls, my father pointed us to the house, about forty rods ahead, the sight of which struck a damp on my spirits, as it appeared to me only an abode of wretchedness. After going to it and taking a general view of the house and the land around, before the team came up, I determined within myself to return to Connecticut; thinking it better to be there to dig clams for my living than to be in such a place. I was disappointed, grieved, vexed, and mad. Though I was some over thirteen years, I cried."

Elias was so disappointed with his new home that he turned around and tried to run back to Connecticut. His father saw him and commanded him to stay in Vermont. Elias, like any other boy who didn't like his new home at first, soon became a real Vermonter, spending the rest of his life here.

Elias had been to school and could read and write when he came to Vermont. He had even been baptized in the Congregational Church. When he was about eight years old his uncle and his mother took him to church to be "sprinkled," as he called it, but Elias, having heard of their plans, decided to run away. The preacher chased him and grabbed him and baptized him anyhow, and to his mother's shame he quickly wiped off the holy water.

In the summer of 1783 they had little to eat, only milk thickened with flour. Clothing was scarce too; he did not own a coat until he was twenty years old. In those hard years many children wrapped straw on their feet because they had no shoes.

Stamps, Money, and New Shoes

Elias probably didn't know it but there was a printing press over in Westminster where Judah Spooner and Timothy Green published a newspaper, *The Vermont Gazette or Green Mountain Postboy*. Anthony Haswell of Bennington, who also printed an early newspaper, was appointed Vermont's first postmaster when the Assembly established five post offices in 1784.

Even if Elias had wanted to write to his old friends back in Connecticut, he couldn't have afforded to. Paper was scarce and costly and the person who received the letter had to pay postage when it arrived by post-rider. Often when families moved away there was never any more communication with the friends and relatives they left behind, because journeys overland were so rough and dangerous. However, a few sturdy souls might travel on winter ice to visit in their former home towns.

Spooner and Green printed Vermont's first official money and one day when some counterfeit, or false, money turned up, the printers were accused. The two men were frightened, for counterfeiters were punished by hanging. But their necks were saved when it was discovered that some dishonest boys who worked in the shop had stolen unfinished bills and forged signatures on them.

Vermont issued copper money too, made by Reuben Harmon from Rupert who built a machine that could make sixty coins a minute, each stamped with the words *Republic of Vermont*. Like Elias Smith's family, nobody had much money. Sometimes not a coin could be found in the entire town, so people often bought supplies and paid their taxes in wheat or animals or other farm products.

One way pioneers made cash money was by selling potash. The tree-covered land had to be cleared to make fields for farming, and all the wood that couldn't be used for buildings was burned, and the wood-ashes were collected.

"Pa, what will you do with all those ashes?" asked a five-year-old girl as she watched her father pile them into a wooden vat he had built.

"You'll see," he smiled.

"Be careful," said her mother to her and her smaller brothers and sisters. "Don't go near the wet ashes. The lye in them will burn you."

The girl watched her parents drain the water that had been poured over the ashes and boil the liquid down in the great iron kettle that they had brought with them to their homestead. The black gum that was left in the boiling pot was packed into a sack for Pa to sell in the nearest big market town.

"They'll ship it far away to Europe for making special soap to wash wool cloth," said Ma. When Pa came home from the week's journey, he had sold forty pounds of potash and brought home a *New England Primer*.

"Now you must learn your letters," he said to his daughter, holding out the little book with its tiny pictures and baffling words. "I will teach you myself come winter, and then next year maybe we'll have a school in town."

The family grew or made almost everything they needed —their own grain and vegetables, and maple sugar; soap, and cloth from flax and wool. If they were prosperous people, they had a cow and chickens and geese.

The children helped make the tallow candles that lit the houses. Home-ground cornmeal was made into mush over kitchen fireplaces, and it was a feast when Pa shot wild game. In 1779, when Vermont was fast filling up with settlers, the Assembly had passed a law that deer could be hunted only six months out of the year, for people were killing wild game too fast.

When the land became settled, shoemakers went from farm to farm and stayed a few days to make and repair shoes for the family. Gossip flew as the shoemaker passed on the news of the other settlers. Many shoemakers would make children's shoes with no difference between left and right: the shoes were soaked in water and the boy or girl, who went barefoot half the year, would put on the wet shoes and wear them until the hard leather took the shape of the aching feet.

"Be thankful you've got shoes at all," said Ma sternly when the children grumbled about the pain caused by their stiff new shoes.

"Yes," agreed Pa. "I hear in the town that Governor Chittenden has proclaimed a Day of Thanksgiving for Thursday the Thirteenth of November this year of 1783. We have much to be thankful for in Vermont. The United States should follow our lead, and set aside a day of thanks."

Vermont, the Fourteenth State

By 1790, the United States had a new Constitution and wanted Vermont to be the Fourteenth State.

"We're getting along all right," said some Vermonters. "We've got eighty-five thousand people here and we don't pay as many taxes as the states do. Let's keep on being an independent republic, free to do as we please."

But the men in the Assembly knew that most Vermonters wanted to be part of the United States. Even New York made friendly advances, by setting up a commission to try to settle the old disputes.

"Vermont isn't getting in until she pays us for some land claims," objected some of the New York legislators.

The Vermont Assembly voted to negotiate with New York and quite peacefully agreed to pay New York her demand for $30,000. All that was left to be done was to vote to ask for admission and to ratify the Constitution of the United States; the Assembly called a convention for that purpose to meet in Bennington in January of 1791. The vote was overwhelming, 105 to 2, in favor of becoming the Fourteenth State. Representatives were chosen to take the news to Congress, which voted unanimously to accept Vermont into the Union.

A few cannon were fired, and here and there high-spirited boys played fifes and drums to lead a march while others lit bonfires when the good news was brought to the towns.

Soon the people elected Senators and Representatives to go to Congress. At last, on March 4, 1791, Vermont became a full-fledged member of the United States of America, the first state to enter the Union after the original thirteen colonies.

6. From Statehood to the Civil War

Some Special People

Matthew Lyon and the New Century

By 1800 Vermont was a busy state with 154,000 people and new leaders in charge. Thomas Chittenden, Ethan Allen, and many of the other Green Mountain Boys were dead, but Matthew Lyon, formerly a Green Mountain Boy and now a member from Vermont to the House of Representatives in Congress, was one of the most talked-about people in the state.

Years before, when Lyon was a teenager, he had run away to America from his home in Ireland. A boy who attracted adventures, he said he was sold "for a pair of stag oxen" by the ship's captain to pay for his passage.

Young Lyon was put to work in Connecticut, and when he was a young man he moved to Vermont with neighbors. He had learned to read, and people found that Matthew's mind was as bright as his red hair. Throughout Vermont's early days he was a soldier and an energetic worker for the state.

When high-tempered Matthew Lyon went to Congress he

began at once to criticize President John Adams for his "kingly manners."

"The Vermont people who elected me are plain farmers, and they don't expect their Representative to put on airs," he said hotly. So he refused to bow and scrape to the President and wrote such sharp letters about it to the newspapers that some people grew equally angry over what they considered Lyon's rude backwoods manners.

Finally he got into a spitting match with another Representative who hit Lyon with a cane. Lyon defended himself with the fire tongs, and the fight was on. The newspapers drew cartoons of the squabble on the floor of Congress and people made up funny songs about him, which made Lyon angrier than ever.

Lyon's letters to the newspapers and his conduct caused some of his enemies to pass laws that enabled them to put him in jail.

"Maybe his opinions and his manners don't please a lot of people, but he has the right to think them and state them if he wants to," said his friends.

"There's no reason to pass special laws just to make a man think like everybody else," said others.

Vermonters rose to his defense, and Lyon was re-elected to Congress. Later the laws were declared unconstitutional. Because of Vermonter Matthew Lyon, freedom of speech and the press was made more certain in all of America. No longer could people be put in prison for their opinions, even if what they thought was not agreeable to other people.

The Story of Fanny Allen

When Ethan Allen had retired from public life he built a house in Burlington for his second wife and young children. His little girl Fanny, named for her mother, was especially gentle and beautiful, so the stories go. One day she was playing by the riverbank when a dreadful monster seemed to appear to her. Fanny was terribly frightened, but she looked up and saw a man with a long white beard who told her not to be afraid.

"Fanny has an imagination as big as her father's," said Mrs. Allen when breathless Fanny reported the incident. And everybody but Fanny forgot about it.

When Fanny was a teenager she asked her mother if she could go to school in Canada to learn French. Ethan Allen was dead by then, and Mrs. Allen was reluctant to give permission, because this was not an ordinary thing for a Vermont girl to do. However, Mrs. Allen and Fanny took a Lake Champlain boat to Montreal, where they looked for a suitable school. When they visited the Hôtel Dieu, a convent school for fashionable young ladies, Fanny fell to her knees and pointed to a picture in the chapel.

"Mother, that's the man who saved me from the monster!" she cried.

Fanny, whose father had believed in a religion based entirely on reason, and whose mother was Protestant, became a Roman Catholic nun in the days when there were few Catholics in Vermont. After Fanny Allen died in the Montreal convent in 1823 she became well known in Canada and Vermont as "the Beautiful Nun." Today her portrait hangs in the State House in Montpelier, and the Fanny Allen Hospital in Burlington was named for her.

Green Mountain Inventors

Vermont has been famous for inventors since the very first patent issued in America, signed by President George Washington, was awarded to a Vermonter in 1791. The man was Samuel Hopkins of Pittsford, who had thought of a better way to make potash.

James Wilson was a boy who loved geography and astronomy. When he saw an English globe in Boston he was so excited that he determined that he would make one himself. He had no idea how to proceed, so he began by carefully carving a round ball of wood, and then drawing on it a map of the world.

That was too crude for this careful young man. After painstaking trials and errors in his Bradford home, he taught himself to make copper engravings of maps which he cut in a special pattern and pasted upon a round mold. Then he removed the paper hemispheres and glued the two halves together to make a lightweight model of the world. His were the first globes made in America, and there was great excitement in 1814 when the scholars in Boston and New York found that a homespun young Vermont farmer could make globes finer than those from Europe.

A Brandon blacksmith, Thomas Davenport, became enchanted with the study of electricity in 1830, a subject that nobody knew much about. Young Davenport thought that magnets and electricity could be used to make a motor. His idea worked, and in 1834 he exhibited a crude electric motor in New York. He continued to improve it and to exhibit newer models, and later he made a small electric train to show how his motor could be used in a practical way. He made an electric press and used it to print a magazine that told about the use of electric power. He even made the first electric piano.

Davenport had various partners who helped him with his work, and he had patents on a number of his inventions. But he was not a businessman, and other people took his ideas and made fortunes for themselves. In fact, the idea for the telegraph was Davenport's. He died poor and obscure, but long after his death he was recognized as one of America's true inventive geniuses.

Samuel Morey of Fairlee invented a paddlewheel steamboat. His first boat was so small that it could only hold two people, but it was able to paddle *against* the current on the Connecticut at a speed of 2 miles an hour. Morey's boat interested Robert Fulton, who Morey felt stole his ideas to get credit as the inventor of the steamboat.

Morey also built an internal-combustion engine, a mechanism which was later to be used in automobiles but attracted little attention in 1826 when it was invented.

Like Davenport, Morey was neither rich nor famous in his lifetime, and he died bitter and broken-hearted. Legends say that one of his ship models lies at the bottom of Lake Morey today, and there are those who claim with a twinkle in their eyes that it rises and sails in the misty moonlight.

Some of America's greatest guns have been made in Vermont. Ashabel Hubbard, who also invented the rotary pump, and his son-in-law, Nicanor Kendall, invented and manufactured famous rifles. Thousands of patents for various devices and machines were issued to Vermont mechanics, especially to people living in Springfield and Windsor.

St. Johnsbury became a famous town when Thaddeus Fairbanks invented scales that could weigh anything from a feather to a railroad train. In 1829 the industrious Fairbanks brothers, who were manufacturing stoves and plows, added

THADDEUS FAIRBANKS

a new line of business: the sale of hemp.

"Unless we can weigh that hemp more accurately, either we or the customer will be cheated," said one of the brothers.

Thaddeus thought deeply about it, and in a short time he came up with a much improved scale, a platform hung by levers. This scale was followed by even better models, and the accurate weighing of products had a great effect on American trade. Thaddeus Fairbanks also invented the process of artificial refrigeration, but he gave the idea away and never made any profit on it.

The remarkable Vermont inventors, and there were hundreds and hundreds of them through the years, taught themselves, for in the 1800's not many people had much technical schooling, and there were few teachers of mechanical science.

ZERAH COLBURN

Zerah Colburn, Unhappy Genius

"That Zerah Colburn is the smartest lad in the state of Vermont," said the people at Cabot. "He already knows more than the school teacher."

In 1810, when Zerah was six years old, his father discovered that the boy could multiply any figures in his head.

"What's 13 times 97?" asked the astonished father, and the child answered "1,261" with no hesitation. He could do anything with figures. All Mr. Colburn could think of was to exhibit Zerah like a dancing bear or a monkey on a string. Nobody bothered to teach him to read or write before his father began showing him around Vermont for money.

"This boy should have the best possible education," said lawyers and college professors who were astonished with the child genius and disturbed at his father's attitude. "We'll pay for his schooling."

But Mr. Colburn refused these offers and took the boy on a tour of the United States and Europe to make a lot of money, putting him in a "curio museum" along with a giant and other abnormal people. But he failed to get rich.

When Zerah was twenty his father died penniless in Europe. Kind people contributed enough money to the bewildered youth to pay his fare home to Cabot, where after an absence of thirteen years his family was not at all glad to see him. Nevertheless, he married, and despite his lack of formal education he taught at Norwich University. His mathematical powers failed as he grew older, however, and he died poor and unhappy when he was still a young man.

Zadock Thompson, a Boy Who Liked to Collect Things

Zadock Thompson was a sickly boy from Bridgewater who grew to be one of the most influential men in Vermont in the middle 1800's. He observed and wrote down Vermont's civil and natural history in a form so readable, and in a book so inexpensive, that all citizens had a chance to learn about their state.

Because he had heart trouble, he could not do farm work, so the legend goes that he sat under a tree reading while the others in the family raked, and hoed, and carried, and harvested. It does not seem to have made him unpopular, though, for Zadock Thompson appears to have been loved by everyone who wrote about him.

Zadock read every book in the community, and he yearned for more. The first natural and civil history of Vermont, written by Dr. Samuel Williams two years before Zadock was born in 1796, did not tell enough to suit the boy, so he began to write down his own observations and make his own collections and classifications of rocks and rivers, feathers and flowers—in fact, he described everything he noticed in his entire environment. Before long he had his brothers and sisters and his neighbor, Phoebe Boyce, helping him sort out details which would one day lead to his own books of natural history.

When he finished the neighborhood school in Bridgewater, he knew he wanted to go to college, but his desire seemed impossible in the hard times of the early 1800's.

"I guess I'll have to use my head since I'm not strong enough to earn money with my body," decided Zadock. And use his head he did. He wrote an almanac, which his sisters sewed for him by hand, and in the summer of 1819 he set out to peddle it. Zadock was so shy and sensitive that it was mortal pain for him to try to sell his book, especially if the customer spoke to him at all curtly. But he sold enough to put by some money for college, and he learned so much about his state that he began planning more ambitious books.

Zadock Thompson did go to college on the money he earned with his almanacs, graduating from the University of Vermont in 1823. Soon he married his neighbor Phoebe, who continued to help him with his enormous collections.

Zadock Thompson taught school, became a minister, and became the state's official naturalist and geologist. He wrote geography, history, and arithmetic books for children, and published a magazine, and wrote a history of Canada. He wrote a history of Vermont which included a natural history, a civil history, and a gazetteer of all the towns in the state. He was a distinguished professor at the University of Vermont for years.

When Zadock Thompson died in 1856 the eager mind of the curious boy who loved the world around him lived on in his books, and in the collections that he willed to the state.

Special Happenings

The State House

It was thirty-one years after Vermont declared herself independent before the state had a permanent capital. The major towns had been bickering ever since 1777 to be named the capital city, but Montpelier finally won out when the townspeople raised $6,000, contributed the land, and built a fine brick hotel to house the legislators.

In 1808 the legislature convened for the first time in the new three-story hall. So many army troops came to escort the Governor and important guests that all the people couldn't get inside. Little boys squirmed between gentlemen's feet, ladies were mashed and pushed, and little girls were lifted to their father's shoulders.

"Put the soldiers out!" came the cry. "We paid for this building."

"We want to see the iron heating-stove!" shouted another. The huge new stove in front of the Speaker's desk on the second floor was being talked about all over the state.

The Governor asked the soldiers to leave, and the crowd pushed in. Onlookers said that legislators began carving their names on the new benches the very first day.

By 1832, when the benches had been whittled until "the holes were too big for putty and paint," the State House had been outgrown. Architect Ammi B. Young drew up plans for a new copper-domed capitol to be built of granite from Barre's famous quarries near by. Teams of oxen hauled great blocks of gray stone, and craftsmen labored for four years to complete the building which Vermonters considered the most beautiful one they had ever seen.

Twenty-one years later, on a cold January evening in 1857 when stiff winds were blowing over the Winooski River, the building caught fire. The firetender had built hot fires in an effort to warm the building because a committee for revising the Vermont Constitution was to meet the next day. The timbers near the furnace got so hot that they burst into flame, and the citizens of Montpelier watched in horror as the fire raced through their beautiful State House and spread to the roof of the church next door, while firemen worked in vain.

The town had a horse-drawn fire engine, but it was so cold that night that water could not be pumped from the river.

"The sea of fire was too much for a dozen of such machines," reported one paper.

"The scene was an awful one," said another.

All the woodwork in the building was burned out, but so well had the architect done his work that the granite walls and portico still stood. Vermont's capitol building was restored and enlarged, and was still as beautiful as ever.

When the building was finished, sculptor Larkin Mead of Brattleboro made a marble statue of Ethan Allen that is still guarding the State House today. Since there was no picture of Allen to guide him, the sculptor had to use his imagination.

Henry Stevens of Barnet, who founded the Vermont Historical Society in 1838, had valuable documents stored in the State House, many of which were lost in the fire.

It was said that as a joke Henry Stevens had paid for many

of the early old manuscripts with Continental money, which of course was worthless at the time. When people heard what he had done, their funnybones were tickled, and they gave him many old letters and records to share with future Vermonters.

Luckily, historians Benjamin Hall and Hiland Hall had copied many of Henry Stevens's papers, so all his important work in gathering historical material was not lost to today's young people.

Smuggling and the War of 1812

There was more than wondering where the Assembly would meet to worry the people in the new state. Pirates and European nations began seizing American ships and kidnapping sailors, and in 1807 President Thomas Jefferson decided to stop foreign trade for a while. Vermont farmers and merchants who shipped potash and wool and lumber to Canada and Europe, mostly by Lake Champlain, said defiantly that they would not stand for this federal order.

"We'll smuggle," they said, "otherwise we'll starve." So ships and rafts kept right on moving through the lake, and people carried Vermont produce openly across the border to Canada. In 1808 federal customs officials tried to stop a smuggler's ship, the *Black Snake,* on the Winooski River. Two customs men were killed in the fight, and one of the smugglers was hanged by order of Vermont's Chief Justice Royall Tyler.

Yet the smuggling continued. Barrels of potash were rolled downhill over the border into Canada, and Smuggler's Notch got its name as a way-station on the smugglers' route.

All the able-bodied men served in the militia in the early

years of Vermont, and once a year in June there was a training day when the men and boys drilled, and the women looked on or cooked for a big celebration afterward. Some of the towns told their military companies to get ready for war with England, whose ships were stopping any American vessels that tried to sail the ocean, and pressing American seamen into the Royal Navy.

In 1812 war against England came, but the people of Vermont, who did not like having their trade stopped, opposed the war. Lake Champlain was fortified, and the British sank some American vessels and even fired some shots in Burlington. By 1814 the situation was so serious that Vermonters rallied their troops at the border and sent some across Lake Champlain to Plattsburg, New York. On September 11, 1814, American ships under twenty-eight-year-old Commodore Thomas MacDonough defeated the British force on Lake Champlain, and brought the war to an end.

Grateful Vermont gave Commodore MacDonough a farm overlooking Lake Champlain, and people went back to trading in peace.

The Runaway Pond

Before the days of electricity, water power turned wheels to grind grain, saw logs, and drive the machinery to card wool and to weave cloth. Even a brook could power a mill if the water was dammed and then allowed to fall on a millwheel and turn it.

The spring of 1810 was a dry one, and all the streams were low.

"See here," said a man at Glover who needed his grain ground, "Long Pond empties into the Lamoille River, but if we cut a channel from Long Pond to Mud Pond, then the water would flow the other way, since Long Pond is higher. That way we could keep our millwheels turning all the time."

The miller agreed, and on one day in June about sixty men from surrounding towns gathered with picks and within a few hours they cut a canal with water just beginning to trickle.

"It will only take a few minutes to finish it off," said the leader. "Let's rest and eat and watch it fill."

Most of the diggers sat down on the hillside to watch. Suddenly there was a flash, and a roar, and a 50-foot wall of water poured out of Long Pond, emptying the lake and crashing down to the valley, carrying away trees, cows, barns, houses, and horses.

Someone ran faster than the flood to get to the mill and snatch the miller out of the path of the torrent. Within four hours Long Pond was no more, for it had all emptied into Lake Memphremagog.

"Tampering with God's work comes to no good," said the local preacher.

"More to the point, there ought to be a law to keep fools from wrecking nature," muttered the people who lost their possessions in the deluge.

The Year of No Summer

In 1816 spring came early, making the farmers happy. But then it began to rain, slowing down the crops until farmers' foreheads were wrinkled in despair. When seeds were finally beginning to come up in late June, a foot of snow fell, and all the seedlings and even the new leaves on the trees were killed. The sheep had just been sheared, and the poor naked

creatures were freezing to death.

"Come, Sukey," said one farmer's wife to her daughter, "take all the bedcovers and sew them into bags."

"Whatever for, Mother?" asked Sukey, who was not very fond of using her needle.

"You'll see," said her mother. Together they made loose bags of the covers and filled them with the freshly cut fleece. Then they wrapped them around the shivering sheep while the younger children laughed at the sight.

Some farmers brought their sheep right into the house, where the animals bleated by the fire, but many died in spite of all the efforts to save them.

In July and August it snowed and froze again. In September, in spite of the private and public prayers of frantic people, a killing frost ended all hopes for any crop.

The people nearly starved to death as it snowed every month in that black year. Children got sick from eating half-green potatoes, sometimes the only food to be had. Food was shipped in from Canada and other states, but people were so discouraged and poor that many decided to leave Vermont.

Daniel Webster Comes to Call

Vermonters were never lukewarm about politics. In 1840 a political rally was planned in Bennington and Windham counties to encourage people to vote for William Henry Harrison to be President of the United States. It was decided to invite Daniel Webster, the most famous speaker in the entire nation, to come to the meeting. Would he accept? Excitement ran high when Webster said "yes."

"Let's have it on Stratton Mountain," said one of the com-

mittee. "There's a three-hundred-acre clearing up there where we can camp."

Statesman and lawyer, Webster was a hero in Vermont because he agreed with the people that slavery was an evil, and that the state's trade should be protected. Nothing was too good for such a man on such a great occasion.

Somebody provided a barouche, an elegant open carriage with a high seat for the driver, and four matched black horses to pull the visitor over the turnpike to Stratton.

"Ma, Ma, look at all the people and horses and the carriages!" squealed astonished children as six thousand people piled through the Arlington turnpike gate. Ma, who was out of sorts because Pa had gone to the rally with his father and brothers, stopped her churning to watch as traffic inched its way toward Stratton Mountain.

Almost that many people were coming from the other direction, with bands marching ahead of town delegations and all the tootling and fiddling making more noise than the mountains had ever heard before.

"I think I shall faint," cried a girl as Mr. Webster's carriage came in sight.

"Don't," advised Granny tartly. "You'll never see the likes again. Keep your eyes open so you can remember it all to tell your children."

When Mr. Webster finally got to the clearing on Stratton Mountain he began his speech with, "Fellow citizens, I have come to meet you among the clouds."

That night the mountainside was studded with campfires as people set up their wigwams, and singing ran like flame from tent to tent. Oh, tales about that convention are still to be heard among old people who heard it from their grandparents!

The Canadian Rebellion

Some of the Tories who fled from Vermont to Canada in the American Revolution had settled near the border. Many of them were among the Canadians who rose up against the British rule in Canada in 1837. When the rebellion was temporarily put down, the Canadian rebels—or "Patriots," as they were called—came over the border to Vermont for help. Vermonters were sympathetic with the problems of the Patriots and collected money to help them, but the United States was supposed to be neutral, so American troops were sent to the Vermont border. There they tried to stop the rebels from entering the state, although many did cross over.

"No matter how sympathetic Vermonters feel, we cannot enter into the local affairs in Canada," said Governor Silas Jennison.

American and Canadian troops caught the rebels between them on the border, and some Vermonters were arrested for trying to rescue Patriots and protect their leaders. However, no Americans were actually imprisoned, and soon reforms took place in Canada that made people on both sides of the border calm down.

What Vermonters Thought

Churches of the Early Years

In the early days people were not supposed to work or travel or play games on Sunday, and the law forbade "shouting, hallooing, screaming, running, riding, dancing, jumping, blowing of horns" near the churches.

In some places there was a town official called a "tithing

man" to see that people behaved in church. Giggling girls, mischievous boys, and sleepy old folks found themselves touched on the head by a foxtail or a sharp prod on the end of the man's stick. Prayers sometimes lasted an hour, with sermons even longer, and the congregation almost froze because there was no heat in the churches. Most people carried heated soapstones or metal boxes of hot coals to keep their feet warm, while children snuggled under layers of animal skins.

The oldest churches had "noon houses," buildings where horses could be kept warm and a fire could be built so people could eat in comfort between the morning and afternoon services. Some people thought it was wicked to have a warm church, but it was all right to make the horses comfortable.

Although the Vermont Constitution said that the Sabbath ought to be observed, and so the people were taxed to pay for the churches, many people were not terribly religious. Finally, some citizens got so angry at being *made* to support and attend churches that they rebelled, and the laws were changed to give people the right to decide the matter for themselves. Almost everybody continued to attend church, though, and the young people all liked the singing schools that were sponsored by the churches.

Rowland Robinson wrote this description of a Quaker meeting when he was a boy: "One warm October day, a big boy, who had come across-lots to meeting, and on the way filled the crown of his hat with thorn apples, fell asleep in his seat, near the door. Every man and boy wore his hat in Quaker meeting. A sudden nod tumbled his hat from his head, and all its contents clattered on the floor, whither he followed and made his exit on all fours, pushing his hat before him."

Free-Thinkers and New Religions

New religions began to spring up in the 1800's in Vermont. People were restless, and since the laws now said that citizens were free to support, or not support, whatever church they pleased, some thought it might be worth looking into new religious ideas.

Hadn't Ethan Allen himself been a dissenter in religious matters? And hadn't a missionary priest, Father Jeremiah O'Callaghan, arrived in 1830 to lead the Roman Catholics in Vermont? His coming shocked some of the old people who had grown up in the tradition of the New England Puritans.

Free-thinking had always been a part of the Vermont frontier. Soon after the Revolution a refugee from Burgoyne's army, a fellow named Dorril, established a sect known as "Dorrilites." They were such strict vegetarians that they would not even wear leather shoes or the skins of animals. Dorril said that the Lord had told him that no human arm could hurt him, but an angry person in the congregation knocked Mr. Dorril to the floor as he stood preaching in the pulpit, and so put an end to that religion.

Another group which people talked endlessly about wore rough clothes and believed that it was sinful to wash themselves. In fact, the story went, over in Woodstock they rolled in the dirt to make themselves holy, thus getting the name "Holy Rollers."

"Up in Hardwick the people are rolling on the floor of the church and yelling and screaming to show their religion," one report said in 1837. Crowds of people went to Hardwick to see them, but other ministers had some of the Holy Rollers arrested for making a disturbance on the Sabbath Day.

It seemed that almost every town had a preacher who felt

called to do something original to show that he could rebel against the old Puritan church customs.

A preacher named William Miller studied the Bible carefully for several years and then predicted that the end of the world would come within a year after March 1843. His idea was picked up by the state's newspapers, and even by national papers. When a crowd gathered at the home of Ira Young in Jamaica for a prayer meeting some of the neighbors became so angry at the disturbance that they threw rocks at the house and at the assembled Millerites, and in the excitement Mrs. Young died of a heart attack.

The Millerites so firmly believed that the world would end as William Miller predicted that they did not take care of their farms or make any plans for the future except to make wings and white robes to wear in Heaven. On the appointed day, many members of the sect climbed up in trees to be nearer to heaven. When Judgment Day failed to come, Millerism died out.

Spiritualism, which attempts to communicate with the spirits of the dead, always interested Vermonters. Just before and after the Civil War there was even a state-wide newspaper devoted to spiritualism. People came from all over the world in the 1870's to see the Eddy family of Chittenden who, it was said, were able to call up spirits from the "other world." All the children in this family were said to have such mysterious powers, which they inherited from their mother.

JOHN
HUMPHREY
NOYES

John Humphrey Noyes, a well-educated man from Putney, founded a religious community whose ideas made the local people so angry that the whole group moved to New York, where they became known as the Oneida Community.

A long-lasting and important religious movement started by a Vermonter is the Church of Jesus Christ of Latter-day

JOSEPH SMITH

BRIGHAM YOUNG

Saints, or the Mormon Church. Joseph Smith of Sharon was its founding prophet in 1830. Brigham Young of Whitingham was the leader who took the Mormons west after the death of Joseph Smith in Illinois, and settled in Salt Lake City in Utah. By 1850, several hundred Vermonters, and many people from the Middle West, had followed them to Utah.

Women and Their Ideas

The religious upheavals of the 1800's calmed down about the middle of the century, but many women who had taken part in the new thinking were restless. They were as well educated as their husbands and brothers, and a number of women were resentful that they could not vote on any matters, not even in school meetings. They were as interested in politics as the men, yet they had no voice.

"Why can't we vote?" they asked each other. It was a bold idea, and most men—and women, too—laughed at it.

The North and the South were disputing with each other about the matter of slavery in the mid-1800's. Slavery had never been allowed in Vermont, but some women said openly that they were tired of working like slaves themselves and that they were sympathetic with the black slaves of the South. When women were admitted to the Vermont Anti-Slavery Society in 1840, it was a great moment for them.

Although divorce was easier for women in Vermont than in most states, a divorced or unmarried woman had a hard time earning a living. Teaching school or laboring in a factory were the main openings for women. Therefore, when a young woman, and a divorced woman at that, became editor of a Vermont newspaper, it was news indeed!

When Clarina Howard was born in West Townshend in 1810 nobody guessed that she would become Vermont's first women's-rights advocate.

"Clarina knows her own mind," said the neighbors as they watched the sturdy little girl grow up.

After being the star pupil in the village school, she went on to the Select Seminary in Townshend, and graduated with honors. Soon she married a young man of the town and moved to New York, where she had three children and taught school as well. The marriage did not work out, so Clarina came back to Vermont with her children and divorced her husband—a daring step in those days.

Bright and energetic, in 1843 she was able to get a job on a Brattleboro newspaper, *The Windham County Democrat,* and she soon married the editor, George Nichols. Before long Clarina Nichols took over the editorship, and through her paper for ten years she worked for the rights of women.

The lot of women was pretty miserable. If a woman owned property when she got married it became her husband's. Women had no right to make decisions about their children, for whatever fathers said was law. Women were not allowed to vote in any elections, although they could attend Town Meeting to cook a dinner.

Mrs. Nichols attacked such problems in her editorials, and through them she persuaded the legislature to pass a law that married women could own property. She even visited the legislature herself to ask the lawmakers to allow women to vote in school meetings.

"I earned the dress I wore, my husband owned it—not of his own free will but by a law adopted by bachelors and other women's husbands," she told them.

The men applauded her. "By Jove, I never thought of women having rights before," some of them said thoughtfully. But more of them laughed at the idea, and the law was not passed. Nevertheless, although Clarina Nichols and her family moved away to Kansas in 1854, the groundwork was laid for the legal rights of women in the state, and in 1880 they were allowed to vote in Vermont towns' school meetings.

Problems for Children and Parents

Until not many years ago, each Vermont town had an "overseer of the poor" to distribute public charity to people who had no families who could care for them—orphans, the very poor, or the handicapped. At first, when a new family moved to town it was "warned out" according to a law which said that if newcomers became paupers they could be sent back where they came from. The towns did not want to take on any new burdens, especially paying for children who might become a lifelong financial responsibility to the taxpayers. For over a century in the larger towns, all the unfortunates—young and old, sane and insane—were housed together in the town "poorhouse" or at the "poor farm," where children often got the worst of it.

Although the warning-out law was changed in 1817, children suffered under other laws. Nothing prevented parents from giving away their children from their often enormous families, and a child's time belonged to its parents. A generous father of 1858 ran this advertisement in a newspaper:

> "I hereby give my son George his time during the remainder of his minority. I shall not claim his earnings hereafter, and all contracts made by him will be binding on him alone."

So George was on his own, for better or worse.

When factories sprang up, boys and girls were employed, and millowners could treat them as they pleased unless the selectmen interfered.

Money was scarce, and fathers could be put in jail if they did not pay their debts, even small ones. In 1831 in Middlebury, ninety-one people were in jail at one time for debt, and five of them owed less than a dollar! Two years later in Burlington, nearly five hundred people were in jail for debt, but only thirteen were in jail for other crimes.

The debtor could go out to work each day to earn money to pay his debt, but he had to sleep in the jail. Many prominent people were put in debtors' prison. A Revolutionary War hero, General William Barton, was in prison for debt for years until General Lafayette, the French nobleman who fought on America's side during the war, heard of his old friend's troubles and sent the money for his release.

In 1838 the debtors' law was repealed in Vermont, as well as in New York and New Hampshire.

Schools and Libraries

The University of Vermont was founded in 1791 as the result of Ira Allen's vision and gifts of money and land, and by 1800 most children had some schooling. However, it was 1867 before a law was passed saying that children from eight to fourteen years old must attend school at least three months a year, and then only if the child had lived in Vermont for a year or more. That same year the legislature passed a law that children under the age of ten could not work in a factory!

Every town had its own independent school system, but most of these public schools were not free. Because the state provided no money for education, each year the town would vote on whether or not to pay for a school. Sometimes a town would vote against paying for a school that year, so parents and good citizens did the best they could to find money to keep a school going.

As for textbooks, if a school had no money to spend for books, the parents either donated volumes that they had at home, or sent none at all.

Almost anybody who could read and write was allowed to teach school. Some teachers were only twelve or thirteen years old, and it was 1845 before the state had superintendents who picked the teachers after a simple examination. There were no public high schools, but those who could afford it attended private academies that were established in larger towns.

In most families, only the youngest ones could have the luxury of going to school, for the older ones had to help with the farm and household chores. There was no school transportation and, as the littlest ones could not walk very far, there were many small neighborhood schools.

There might be eight or ten schools in a town, all one-room buildings, which a dozen or so students might attend in a year. The teachers were paid about a dollar a week in the middle of the 1800's, and were "boarded around" in the students' homes.

Some Vermont school children today have discovered the cellar holes of old schools. Under the supervision of the

teacher some students have made "archeological digs" in them, discovering bits of slate and window glass, rock foundations, and rusty buckets. Such remains bring back pictures of the past when children sat on backless benches learning reading, writing, and ciphering from the blackboard, and keeping warm in winter with a wood-burning "pot belly" stove, and using a privy in back of the schoolhouse.

The first blackboard in America was used by a Vermonter, Samuel R. Hall of Concord Corner. He simply mounted on a wall a much larger piece of slate than the students used at their desks to write on, for back then paper was scarce and therefore expensive. In 1823, Mr. Hall also opened there the nation's first normal school, for training teachers.

Sometimes families with young people who could not afford to go to school would swap teenagers to work in another family, and learn new ideas. Most often they learned that people who didn't work didn't survive, a fact that went for children, too.

Although many Vermonters who owned books had always shared them, in 1791 Brookfield was the first town to establish a formal library association. Soon Montpelier followed with a two-hundred-volume library, but it was not for just anybody to use. In Peacham the first children's library, the Juvenile Library Association, was formed in 1810, and by 1825 the State Library was established. In 1875 there were seven town public libraries in the state, and many towns had private libraries or "reading circles" where books were exchanged.

Vermont was the fifth state in the Union to provide free libraries when the legislature appointed a Library Commission in 1894. Within two years there were sixty free libraries in Vermont, and today books are available to every person in the state.

How Vermonters Lived

Vermont Roads

"We need roads," the people fumed as the population grew. "We could build more towns if we had roads."

So in 1779, when Vermont was only two years old, the legislature passed a law requiring the towns to maintain and survey their roads and build new ones if possible. Every able-bodied man had to donate three or four days' work each year to keep the town's roads fit to be used.

In 1785, Colonel Enoch Hale built a suspension toll bridge across the Connecticut River at Bellows Falls. People walked or rode horses many miles to see this wonder, which connected Vermont and New Hampshire.

Colonel Hale then built from his bridge a toll turnpike that finally led to Rutland, and other enterprising people built roads to connect with it. Gradually Vermont developed a turnpike system that allowed stagecoaches and four-wheeled wagons to bump from town to town.

A farmer could make a little money by building a stretch of toll road, and the children of the family took turns guarding it so nobody could sneak through without paying. Of course, some dishonest people tried to get around the toll-gates, sometimes cutting secret roads called "shunpikes" around the toll station, causing a few chasings and beatings.

In 1825 the Marquis de Lafayette, the French general who had so gallantly served the United States in the Revolution, dazzled many Vermont towns when he traveled on the turnpikes in his coach drawn by six cream-colored horses. School children turned out to sing to him, and great feasts and balls were held for him. Wherever he went he was accompanied by ten other carriages filled with distinguished people.

Inns were built along the main routes, and travel was an exciting but uncomfortable adventure for the few who tried it. Rocks, holes, ditches, and dust faced the stagecoach patrons, but nevertheless it was possible to buy a ticket from larger Vermont towns to Albany, Montreal, Boston, or New York even in the early 1800's. Although it was cold in the stagecoaches, the best traveling was in winter after the snow was rolled to make it smooth.

Smooth roads are a quite modern invention, and it was the end of the century before Vermont had a state highway department, and even later than 1900 before the first paved roads were built.

Taking in Boarders

"Do you mean the Vermont legislature is going to meet *here* —here in Danville?" Henry Little heard his mother cry out excitedly one day in 1805. Ten-year-old Henry, busy with chores near the kitchen door, put down the water bucket and ran into the house to listen.

"Yes," his father was saying, "even the new inn isn't big enough to take care of all the members."

Mrs. Little stood thinking a moment. "Mr. Little, why don't we take boarders ourselves? That way we can put by a little money."

Many years later Henry Little wrote about the exciting autumn when his family opened their house to legislators in the days before Montpelier was the permanent capital and every town wanted to be chosen for the meeting of the General Assembly.

The members of the legislature arrived on foot or horse-back, for there were no four-wheeled vehicles in the area. The boarders at the Little house were all Baptists or Methodists, Henry reported, and they called each other "Brother."

"Our table fare was very good," Henry Little wrote, "but it was limited to a less variety of edibles than we now have, there being no cultivated fruit except a few apples and currants. . . . Some people ate from wooden bowls, with wooden spoons, but iron and pewter spoons were generally used. Trenchers, or wooden plates, very neatly turned from hard wood, in size and shape of earthen plates, were much in use . . . because they did not dull their knives."

The Littles had no carpets or rugs. Instead, the split-log floors were covered with clean white sand, and every morning Mrs. Little made fancy patterns in the sand with her broom.

Henry listened while the legislators talked about laws as they ate. There were not many jails in the state, so punishment was quick—a public whipping, or a few hours of standing with head and arms locked in a wooden pillory.

Henry carried slops, chopped wood for the fireplaces, held horses, brushed boots, carried water, and listened to every word he could overhear from these men who came from such faraway places as Rutland, Brattleboro, and Middlebury. No boy had ever had a more exciting three weeks.

When it was all over, Henry listened with a woebegone face as they made farewell speeches. Henry wrote: "Brother Bailey had succeeded in raising a sum of money which he had been delegated to deliver to me as a testimonial of their high appreciation of my considerate attentions to them; and then O wonderous delight! my hand received a bright silver coin of the value of six and one-fourth cents. I regret to say that I was so overcome by that affecting scene that I was wholly unable to offer a becoming response."

Marvels of the Age

Since hard work was always the order of the day in Vermont, the people used their heads to invent labor-saving devices to save their backs.

Grinding grain was one of the first necessities, so pioneers made "plumping mills" in hollowed-out stumps, using a rock tied to a limber sapling to pound the grain. Children were put to work to make the rock go up and down, up and down, to crush the grain into meal or flour. This work was so tiresome that people cheered when a village mill was set up. Most towns even gave the land to a man who would build a mill.

Children worked endless hours carrying water to the kitchen and to the animals. Nobody knows for sure, but it may have been some clever farm youth who thought up the "water ram" that saved many hours of carrying heavy buckets.

"Here's how it will work, Pa," said some young man who might have studied math and physical science at an academy or one of Vermont's colleges. "If we dam the brook, and put in a tiny pipe no higher than the head of the stream, it can force the water to a cistern outside the kitchen and fill it up, slow and steady. Then when Ma wants water in the stone sink, or if we need to water the cows we can let it flow by gravity through a pipe."

Pa studied the idea, secretly pleased with his son. "Might work. You always were smarter than hardworking, son."

The boy thought a minute. "Come to think about it, when

we get the water to the sink why not pipe the extra water right to the pigpen watering trough? Then we won't have to carry *any* water."

Ma was overcome with the invention. Women's work had become lighter with the invention of carding machines to comb fibers for spinning and weaving, and power looms were beginning to weave cloth, saving endless hours at home looms.

As early as 1810 paper was made in Vermont, as well as glass, pig iron, pottery, and bricks. Cast-iron heating stoves were being manufactured near Brandon around 1820, and before long they would be adapted for cooking, too. When the stoves reached the villages the men, women, and children would gather to touch and admire these marvels, which meant the warmth that every family longed for.

In 1836 matches, or "lucifers," were invented—although they didn't reach Vermont right away. When they did, if a fire went out it was no longer a family crisis that meant going to the neighbor's house, sometimes miles away, for a shovelful of coals, or laboriously striking flint to make sparks on tinder. But nobody wasted matches, of course. They were just for an emergency, and not everybody had them by any means.

Breweries and distilleries were in most towns, not that Ma approved of them. She had more time to think now about what she liked and didn't like, and more time to visit with other woman who were beginning to talk among themselves about the evils of too much alcohol. There were men who

agreed and began to talk of passing laws to control the sale of rum and whiskey.

Blacksmiths were the most important men in town, some thought. Smart, too, for they invented all kinds of things to make life easier. Over in Windsor, blacksmith Lemuel Hedge patented a device for ruling lines on paper that made bookkeeping and writing in a ledger much neater.

There was a power machine made in East Poultney that used a horse or a goat on a treadmill to turn a wheel to power a saw—or, it was rumored, even a machine for washing clothes, although Ma could hardly believe that. Why, they might even invent a sewing machine next!

A son liked to astonish his parents with stories of inventions. "I heard that the rotary pump that Ashabel Hubbard invented is being manufactured in the prison at Windsor," said the boy. "They pay the prisoners twenty-five cents a day to work."

"Maybe prisoners can pay off their debts that way," said Pa. "A good idea."

So families talked of the new marvels of the age.

"You won't believe this," laughed the boy, who had picked up great knowledge in the outer world. He almost choked on the joke he was going to share. "They say that President John Quincy Adams has set up a mechanical privy in the White House in Washington."

"Mechanical privy!" gasped his mother. "No, I don't believe it."

"It's true," chuckled the boy. "They named it a water closet, but some people say they call it 'John Quincy's privy' or the 'John Quincy' or just the 'John' in Washington, because the President had it installed."

"Now, that is not at all polite," said his mother. "I'm sure they'll never have such a device in Vermont."

The Morgan Horse

"A good horse has to be handsome, docile, strong, and fast, and be good breeding stock," said men in 1795. In Randolph a singing-teacher named Justin Morgan needed a saddle horse, and since his cousin in Springfield, Massachusetts, owed him a sum of money, Morgan agreed to accept an undersized colt and an older horse as part payment.

Morgan, who named the colt "Figure," got sick and couldn't ride him much. "I suppose I could rent Figure out to Robert Evans," Morgan decided. "He wants a horse for clearing land. He'll pay me fifteen dollars a year for the use of the colt, and I need the money."

Justin Morgan's horse developed such leg and chest muscles from the hard work of land clearing that when Evans rode him in some of the races that farmers were forever getting up at the end of the work day, little Figure always won. Figure's name had changed a time or two, and by now he was generally called Justin Morgan's Horse, and finally simply Justin Morgan, for Justin Morgan the man had died.

The horse Justin Morgan lived to be thirty-two years old —a great age for a horse—with a number of different owners, and stories of his strength and his beauty and his speed and his good temper grew until he was famous all over the state. Nobody took very good care of him, but not long after he died, horse breeders realized that his descendants had the good qualities of their legendary ancestor. Morgans became famous for their strength, speed, beauty, and courage, as well as for their intelligence and gentle dispositions.

Morgan horses, one thousand of them, showed their worth in the Civil War as cavalry mounts, when the First Vermont Regiment rode them into seventy-five battles and skirmishes.

"Our Morgans are the best horses in the entire Union

Army," said Vermont soldiers as their special horses aroused the admiration of other cavalry troops. Two hundred of the horses survived the war, and many of them returned to Vermont along with the veterans.

The Morgan became America's first native breed of horse. Today the University of Vermont has the Morgan Horse Farm at Weybridge, near Middlebury, and breeds the horses on nine hundred acres donated by Colonel Joseph Battell, a man who loved Morgans.

Merino Sheep

When William Jarvis, an American sea captain, was representing the United States in Lisbon, the capital of Portugal, in the uneasy days of the War of 1812, he noticed the flocks of hardy merino sheep all over the countryside.

"Ah," he said to himself, "what fine wool these sheep have —they would be splendid for my farm in Vermont."

The merino sheep came originally from Spain, Portugal's next-door neighbor, and Mr. Jarvis was able to ship three thousand of the sheep to America, three hundred of which went to his farm at Weathersfield.

The sheep thrived and multiplied in Vermont's climate, and he sold them at reasonable prices to the farmers around him. Vermont began to be so prosperous that by 1840 there were six sheep for every person in the state. Woolen mills sprang up in towns with good water power, and farm boys and girls left home to go to work in them.

The sheep boom lasted only a few years in Vermont because farms in the West with great areas of grazing land could produce wool at lower prices, and many Vermonters lost their money when the sheep herds disappeared from the landscape.

Water Travel

"Steamers are just the thing for Lake Champlain," said eager promoters when steamboats were becoming more frequent after the War of 1812. Thereafter for a century, passengers and freight passed up and down Lake Champlain, often carried in splendid vessels made in towns along the lake.

Shipping people studied the map and saw that a canal could expand the water traffic enormously. In 1823 the Champlain Canal was built to connect Lake Champlain with the Hudson River so people and goods could get to New York by ship. Two years later the Erie Canal made it possible to go all the way to the western Great Lakes by transferring to a special canal boat.

In 1802 America's first canal for navigation and a set of locks were built at Bellows Falls in hope that vessels could travel the length of the Connecticut River. Before steamboats were available, flatboats or rafts were made on the upper Connecticut River and poled or drifted south, where at the end of the voyage the raft would be broken up and sold for timber.

Oxen would pull the rafts through the locks; if the current was slow, the deckhands would pole the vessel along. There were no cabins on these crude boats, so the men would sleep ashore at night. River towns were lively places with inns and entertainments for the river travelers.

In 1826 the steamer *Barnet* was built, but the big boat could not get through the locks, and the river was too shallow in spots. Therefore the *Barnet* never got two-thirds up the state to the town for which it was named, although newspapers of the day report great celebrations as the vessel inched its way up to Bellows Falls before it had to stop.

Although a few smaller boats got as far as the town of

Wells River, the Connecticut River, which had been the main eastern Vermont travel route for the Indians and early settlers, was a disappointment for commercial transportation. But on the other side of the state, Lake Champlain kept communications with Canada alive, and opened up the expanding West to Vermont trade and travel.

The Coming of the Railroads

The Central Vermont Railroad was chartered in 1843, and when the first section of track from Bethel to White River was completed in 1848, three cars were run over the twenty-seven miles and caused excitement such as the state had never seen.

Families came in wagons to see the iron monster charge by. Horses ran away, children screamed, women fainted, and men got drunk with joy. A year later a train of three hundred passengers from Burlington met a train of one thousand passengers from Boston at Windsor, and the town had a great display of fireworks to celebrate. Never had there been such a festival!

There was a rivalry among the many railroad companies. The Rutland & Burlington company beat Central Vermont in a great race to lay tracks to Burlington. Railroad-builders imported many laborers to lay the tracks, for Vermont men were mostly busy with their farms. Strong men used muscles and brawn to dig and hammer, blast and heave, to get the tracks laid. The influence of the railroads was felt in all parts of the state.

"Hey, folks, look who's home!" cried a young man's voice at the kitchen door at supper time.

"Heavens, how did you get here?" asked his mother and

father. Smaller brothers and sisters gathered around.

"Have you been expelled from college?" his father demanded sternly.

"Of course not," laughed the boy. "School closed for a few weeks because of a mumps epidemic. I've had them, remember, so I paid my fare on the train by stoking wood for the engineer, and he let me off the train here, down below the back pasture. Didn't cost me a penny. Didn't you hear the whistle toot?"

Farmers with woodlots by the tracks could cut and sell enough to the wood-burning trains to pay for such luxuries as sending a bright son to college.

Fortunes were made and lost in Vermont railroads, and so important were the railroad officials that three presidents of three railroads became governors of Vermont.

In 1849 newspapers carried the astonishing news that the Rutland & Burlington railroad would give a free ride to anyone who wanted to visit Burlington.

"I'm going," declared fathers, sons, and grandfathers. Even some of the ladies went along, carrying ample baskets of bread and apple butter and hard-boiled eggs and pork pies. Firecrackers were shot off and crowds along the way watched the lucky ones chug by.

"We'll never find a room," said discouraged passengers when they finally got to Burlington. All the hotels, boarding-houses, and even private homes were filled. Some people hired buggies and rode miles out of town to find lodging.

Engines on some of the railroads had names like *Stranger* or *Red Bird*, and the people were proud of their trains. Towns vied with each other to have the railroads come to them, and often the citizens voted to lend the companies money, for people believed with all their hearts that the railroads would guarantee prosperity.

Emigration

The same restlessness that brought people to Vermont took away their descendants when roads, ships, and railroads made travel easy. Vermont boys who had seen their parents worried by political problems, debts, and crop failures, looked at the opening West and said, "I'm leaving, Pa. There's good land and high wages out there."

And the daughters, not wanting lives like their mothers', read advertisements in Western papers for school teachers and boarded the train, scared to death and clutching a carpetbag of books and home-made clothes. Forty-five Vermont women became foreign missionaries between 1830 and 1840, going to such faraway places as Siam, Hawaii, and Burma.

Whole families left in covered wagons or trains, taking with them Vermont's special brand of stern ideas, willingness to work hard, and respect for education. The Great Emigration, as it was called, began with a trickle about 1820 that became a flood by 1850 when the gold fields of California lured away more than eleven hundred Vermont farm boys who were tired of slopping the pigs.

When people left home, their families wanted pictures of them. A few portrait painters had worked in Vermont, but when a new and inexpensive process of making real likenesses on metal plates, called daguerreotypes, came to Vermont, it was the fashion to have a picture made. By 1850 photographers, usually in carts parked on town streets or at fairs, could make quick pictures of young men in short jackets and caps, or of girls in tight-waisted, full-skirted dresses and fetching bonnets.

"Why did you leave home?" asked one homesick girl of another as they sat on the train together.

"Because my granny used to tell me tales of pioneering to

Vermont when she was my age. I wanted to try it, too. Vermont is too tame now."

"I know," said the other. "The stories they told me when I was a little girl have made me restless all my life."

By the decade before the Civil War, 96,000 Vermonters left the state. Strangely enough, though, the total population did not drop. In fact, it had increased by 22,000 since 1840, giving Vermont 314,000 citizens in 1850.

Something new was certainly happening in Vermont—but that is another story.

7. Vermont
and the Civil War

Anti-Slave Vermont

From the start, Vermonters hated slavery and the first thing they did to prove it was to outlaw slavery in Chapter I, Article 1 of the state's Constitution in 1777.

By the middle of the 1800's, thousands had joined anti-slavery societies, giving money, scarce as it was, to the anti-slavery cause. Ministers preached against slavery, and citizens even left Vermont to try to stop its spread into the newly settled territories in the West. They elected men to Congress who spoke out so loudly against it that Vermont became famous as an anti-slave state.

Vermonters angrily opposed the Mexican War when the United States took Texas from Mexico, for they feared it would extend slavery. However, Vermont soldiers obeyed when the army called them to the war in 1846.

Although the federal government said slave owners could legally capture runaway slaves anywhere in the United States, Vermont made laws to protect slaves who reached her borders. Of course, a state cannot pass laws that conflict with federal laws, but Vermont made it illegal for slave-

133

catchers to take slaves out of the state without a trial. Even federal agents found that Vermont courts made it almost impossible to remove a captured slave.

The Underground Railroad

Slave owners still tried to kidnap slaves from Vermont, and men hired to catch slaves lurked about hoping to get a rich reward for capturing a valuable runaway. Freedom-loving Vermonters entered into a bold secret scheme called the "Underground Railroad" to help runaway slaves who had heard that Vermont was a safe place.

Exhausted, terrified slaves often arrived at the southern Vermont border after following the banks of streams night after night. Waterways were safest, for wading in water would throw bloodhounds off the scent, and a lucky slave might find a raft to make the trip easier, even though he had to pole upstream.

There were two main routes of the Underground Railroad in Vermont that operated for more than thirty years, one from Bennington up the west side of the state and one from Brattleboro up the east side. Houses friendly to runaways were known as "stations." Workers in the Underground took slaves under a load of hay or perhaps even hidden in a trunk to the next station, and so on to Canada and freedom.

Rowland E. Robinson from Ferrisburg, whose Quaker father was an early leader in the Underground Railroad, wrote of daring adventures in rescuing slaves and getting them to safety. His parents had a room over the kitchen where slaves could be hidden in a warm place. Children in the family knew that they must never speak of the noises from the attic, or of wagons arriving in the middle of the night, or of the plates of food that were mysteriously carried up the back stairs.

By the eve of the Civil War slaves dared to ride openly on the trains or boats in Vermont because they knew they were among friends. Some slaves stayed in Vermont, but most of them went to Canada. In 1852 there were thirty thousand black people living in Canada, many of whom had come through Vermont.

When Ezra Brainerd, who was later to become a famous botanist and president of Middlebury College, was a little boy in St. Albans, he helped runaway slaves to escape. He wrote of his adventures:

"Often these fugitive slaves were kept overnight at our house, and I was told to be up early and take them in our carryall [wagon] . . . The poor creatures seemed to suffer badly from the cold, and I recall hearing one of them pray 'Lord, don't let [me] freeze to death so near freedom!' When we reached the iron post that marked the Canada line they would all jump out and shout in ecstasy, 'Thank the Lord, now we'se freemen.'"

Underground Railroad stations covered the state, and today people still find in old houses concealed rooms or false chimneys where slaves were hidden. Often the present owners do not even understand what these hidey-holes were for, because the operation was so secret that it was not openly discussed or written about in the newspapers or books of the period. Even later history books have not said much about Vermont's best-kept secret.

Vermont Goes to War

"Abe Lincoln, hurrah for Lincoln! Abe's our man!" cried people at torchlight parades in Vermont when the news that Abraham Lincoln had been elected President was telegraphed to Vermont in 1860. News traveled fast after the beginning of telegraph service in 1848!

"He opposes slavery in the territories in the West, and he aims to protect our industries, and he's for free homesteads," said the Vermonters, who had voted for him overwhelmingly.

When historians look back on that year they wonder why Vermonters were not more concerned about war when, a few days after the election of Lincoln, South Carolina seceded from the United States and was followed in a few days by other Southern states to set up the Confederate States of America.

Vermonters were more concerned when Lincoln, on his way to Washington for his inauguration, barely escaped assassination. It was discovered that there was a plot to kill Lincoln and seize the federal government. When Lincoln took over as President on March 4, 1861, he had a divided country on his hands.

Vermont had still not alerted the state militia. The old laws that required all able-bodied men to drill on June Training Day had been done away with fifteen years earlier, leaving in the state only twenty-two volunteer companies, most of which did not even have guns. But when the Confederates captured Fort Sumter, a United States base in South Carolina, Vermont woke up.

On April 14, 1861, the news of the fall of Fort Sumter and Lincoln's call for troops exploded through Vermont. Lincoln wanted seventy-five thousand volunteers. It was war!

A private telegram to Governor Erastus Fairbanks from President Lincoln said: "Washington is in grave danger. What may we expect from Vermont? A. Lincoln."

"Vermont will do its full duty," telegraphed the Governor in reply.

And it did. Governor Fairbanks immediately called a special session of the legislature, while people excitedly read every scrap of news in the papers. Long angry at the slave-owning South, legislators piled into Montpelier within eight days and were met by a thirty-four-gun salute from the same cannons that had saved Vermont at the Battle of Bennington in 1777.

"Make it a million," cried one legislator when the committee reported that half a million dollars was needed to raise troops and pay them. And the legislature agreed, voting a sum greater than any other state raised in proportion to population.

When someone, fired with patriotism, suggested that they rise and sing the Star-spangled Banner, they found out that nobody could sing it. But when the evening session began a choir filled the gallery and sang the anthem for the legislators, who were better at making laws than at singing.

Within four days two regiments were authorized by Vermont although Lincoln had asked the state for only one regiment of seven hundred eighty men. Money was raised not only for troops but also as extra pay and relief for families of soldiers. In almost every town flags were raised and public meetings set up means for recruiting soldiers. The colleges formed military companies, banks lent money, and rich men pledged their fortunes.

West Point graduate Colonel John W. Phelps of Brattleboro commanded the First Regiment of Vermont Volunteers. Flags, speeches, bands, and crowds sent off citizen soldiers at railroad stations where trains chugged in to take the volunteers to Camp Fairbanks in Rutland, where the first troops gathered.

It was so cold in Rutland that water froze in the tents, and high winds and rain gave a taste of what was to come. Nevertheless, spirits were high when the special twenty-car train left on May 9, 1861, for Virginia. The train drew into New York City the next morning and the new Green Mountain Boys marched down Fifth Avenue, sporting evergreen sprigs in their hats.

Eventually Vermont had seventeen regiments, three companies of sharpshooters, and one regiment of cavalry. In addition, more than six hundred Vermonters served in the Navy.

Some of the young soldiers thought that the war was going to be an exciting get-together like the old June Training Days their fathers had told them about. But it wasn't. It was one of the deadliest, saddest struggles in history. And it was a disaster for Vermont, who proportionately gave more in men and money than any other Northern state.

By the time the war ended in 1865 Vermont had sent nearly 35,000 men out of her population of 315,000. More than 5,000 of these men were killed and another 5,000 were disabled. The state spent nearly ten million dollars, estimated to be more than the entire amount spent on Vermont's government from 1777 to 1860.

Vermont troops fought with distinction from Virginia to Louisiana and were especially important at the decisive Battle of Gettysburg in July of 1863, where the Vermont Brigade had staggering losses.

Drummer Boys

Teenage boys enlisted with the consent of their parents—and sometimes without it—and many of them died in heavy fighting. Boys under sixteen could go as drummers.

Willie Johnson of St. Johnsbury, Company D, Third Regiment, clung to his drum when Vermont troops were forced to retreat in Virginia. Older soldiers threw away their gear to escape, but Willie kept his head and held on to his drum. When troops finally assembled again after a week of rout, he drummed for the Division parade. This was reported to Washington, and Willie was awarded a medal for his faithfulness and pluck by the Secretary of War.

Another drummer boy, Henry Davenport of Roxbury, was only eleven years old when he went to war with his father, who was wounded at the Battle of Lee's Mill in Virginia. Henry pulled his father to a safe spot from the stream where he fell. When the boy was returning to the stream for a cup of water for his father, a bullet knocked it from his hand. Henry escaped unhurt.

At the same battle another drummer boy named Julian Scott, of Johnson, went twice across the stream to rescue wounded. An observant lad, he remembered small details, and when he grew up to become a noted artist, he made celebrated paintings, including the one of the Battle of Cedar Creek which hangs today in the State House.

The Sleeping Sentinel

Young Private William Scott of Groton was found asleep at his sentry post. Found guilty, he was sentenced to be shot.

"'Tain't fair," said his friends hotly. "Willie was a good

fellow. He's stayed up all night the night before with a sick comrade, and he's had picket duty for two nights before that."

"A soldier can't last forever without sleep," muttered another. "Let's get up a petition."

Willie was in the guardhouse awaiting execution, the first man in the United States army to get sentenced to death for the offense. Hundreds of names piled up on the petition asking for mercy for their friend.

"Chaplain Parmalee's taken it to Washington, Willie," his comrades whispered to him through the bars. "President Lincoln won't let you die."

When the petition reached Abraham Lincoln on the day before the scheduled execution, he telegraphed an order to the camp not to shoot the soldier, expecting the routine military response. But when Lincoln got no answer he couldn't sleep. He ordered his carriage, and driving as fast as he could for ten miles, the President reached the camp a little before midnight.

"Yes, sir," said the startled guards when the President of the United States arrived on his humane midnight mission.

The next morning Scott was taken from his cell by a silent guard who led him to the parade ground where a firing squad was drawn up.

Scott said nothing, but he was deadly pale, ready for death. And then a voice began to read Lincoln's order that Scott was pardoned and was to be returned to duty.

Cheers for the young soldier and cheers for President Lincoln rocked the camp as Private William Scott returned to his company, a free man.

The St. Albans Raid

The Confederacy needed money, and also wanted to stir up trouble between the United States and Canada, a combination that made Vermont become the scene of the only Confederate military action in New England.

Tuesday was market day in St. Albans, when the streets were crowded with farmers bringing their butter to town to be shipped to Boston on the special refrigerated railroad cars. Therefore Wednesdays were dull lazy days for the town, especially on Wednesday in October of 1864 when people were thinking of hunting and of their hopes that the war would soon be over.

Nobody paid much attention to the unusual number of visitors who were registered at the local hotels on that 19th of October. Nobody even noticed that the strangers all spoke with Southern accents.

Nobody knew it, but Bennett Young and twenty-five other men who had arrived in groups of twos and threes on the train from Montreal were Confederate soldiers, posing as salesmen and horse-buyers.

At three in the afternoon when bank clerks were drowsy and few people were on the streets, Young stepped to the porch of his hotel and shouted, "In the name of the Confederate States, I take possession of St. Albans."

The few astonished townspeople on the streets were held at gunpoint, and the raiders entered St. Albans' three banks in a well-laid plan that went without a hitch. The raiders packed more than $200,000 of loot into bags, and then they all jumped on horses which they had led from the local livery stables, and headed for Canada.

No bank employees had been killed, but a stranger in town was hit by a wild bullet and died. Another man, believing that the raiders were insane or joking, refused to stop and was wounded.

A soldier home from war led a chase to the Canadian border. The raiders escaped, but they dropped some of the money. Later most of the men and money were seized by the Canadian government, and after a long time the banks got some of the money back. The end of the war came before the two governments reached an agreement over what to do about the fugitives, and the raiders were not punished enough to suit the people of St. Albans.

After the raid the telegraph operator abandoned his office in the excitement. When Governor John G. Smith, hearing that the town had been attacked, was unable to get a message from St. Albans, it was assumed that the town had been overthrown, and the rumor flew all over Vermont that the Confederates had destroyed it entirely!

Hospitals for Soldiers

Before the Civil War, Vermont had three medical schools—at Castleton, Woodstock, and Burlington—giving the state more than enough doctors to supply her regiments and to work in the Army Medical Bureau as well.

Dr. Elisha Harris of Westminster was a doctor who was concerned about the poor medical care and living conditions of the soldiers, whose wretched food and miserable housing were a disgrace. More soldiers were dying of disease than in battles, so he helped found the Sanitary Commission to help soldiers keep healthy.

"Vermont's clean air is better than medicine," he said.

He and other doctors arranged to have military hospitals set up in Burlington, Montpelier, and Brattleboro. The soldiers got well so fast that it amazed everyone.

"It's a miracle," said authorities in Montpelier when more than six hundred of the thousand soldiers brought to Vermont hospitals recovered in the first year of the experiment.

Vermont took better care of her men than other states did. When soldiers could not be brought home for recovery, the state sent hospital commissioners to the field hospitals to see that Vermont soldiers had decent care.

Vermont Nurses

"I want to serve my country, too," said Vermont women who were inspired by England's famous nurse, Florence Nightingale. They heard, too, of New England's Dorothea Dix and Clara Barton, women who were trying to organize female nursing help for army hospitals.

The Army Medical Bureau was scornful of the offers made by the women. This was before the days of trained nurses, and shocked doctors thought women in hospitals would faint or be undependable, or even be downright nuisances.

"Hospitals are no place for decent women," said most doctors.

But Dr. Elisha Harris knew that women like the ones he had grown up with in Vermont could save many lives. Because of him the Sanitary Commission welcomed nurses, and before the war was over there was even a bureau of nursing headed by Dorothea Dix.

There are no records to tell how many Vermonters were among the 3,200 women who served as nurses in the Civil War, for the men who wrote the history books did not mention them. The stories of a few have come down to us, giving only a small peep into the lives of these daring women.

Putting aside their hoopskirts and donning plain cotton work dresses, Estelle S. Johnson and Lydia A. Wood, from an unidentified "little country village shut in by the mountains of Vermont," enlisted as nurses and served with their husbands in the Vermont Fourth Regiment. Later Mrs. Johnson wrote of being sworn in at Brattleboro in the presence of Governor Fairbanks, who pleaded with them not to go. But they got on the train with the troops and went south to Washington and the Virginia battlefields. Mrs. Wood died of fever, the first Vermont woman to lose her life for the Union.

Amanda Colburn of West Glover was a hospital matron with the Vermont Third Regiment, and Fanny Titus-Hazen from Vershire, in spite of being considered far too young, was allowed to go along with her brothers. At first, most nurses got no pay at all, but finally the government agreed to pay forty cents a day to some of them.

Before the Civil War, in New England nursing was a home art that girls learned from their mothers. There were few hospitals in those days in America, but in Canada, where many Roman Catholic nuns were dedicated to caring for the sick, hospital care was far better. After the Civil War Vermont girls heard about nursing schools that were being established in big cities, and some of them got on the train and went there to become professional nurses.

A Romantic Story

In the midst of the unhappiness in the Civil War was at least one story with a happy ending.

"Must you go to war, Henry?" asked Mrs. Henry Bedell of Westfield in August of 1862.

Henry looked out the window at his fields, just ripening in the August sun, and heard the happy voices of his three children in the yard.

"I won't be drafted," he said, "but I feel a moral compulsion to go. I hope you can understand, and manage."

"I can manage, and I think I understand," said his wife quietly.

So Henry Bedell enlisted as a corporal in the Eleventh Vermont Volunteers, and he kissed his family goodbye and left.

"I have been promoted to lieutenant," wrote Henry Bedell to his wife, who was struggling to keep the farm going without a man on the place. "I will soon be going into the battlefront in Virginia. Pray for me."

While this was happening in Vermont, down in Virginia J. L. E. Van Metre was bidding farewell to his young wife.

"Old Dick Runner and the other servants can help you manage the farm, Betty. I must go and serve the Southern cause."

It was near the Van Metre plantation that Lieutenant Henry Bedell met the Confederates in battle in September of 1864. Moving with a small advance unit, Henry Bedell was gravely injured.

"He's dead," said a comrade. But so strong was Bedell's will to live that he forced himself to speak and told the soldier how to put on a tourniquet to stop his bleeding.

"Now make a stretcher out of that blanket and carry me to safety," said Bedell. "I refuse to die on a Southern battlefield."

The soldiers carried the Lieutenant to the nearest field hospital.

Half-conscious, he heard the surgeons talking about him. "If we don't cut off his leg he'll die."

"Probably he'll die if we do, but he has a chance if we amputate," said another.

Once more Henry Bedell took charge of his life. "Cut my leg off," he ordered through gritted teeth. "I want to live to return to my Vermont farm."

The leg was removed, but nobody but Henry himself thought he had a chance to survive. Even he began to lose hope when the enemy troops got so close that the field hospital had to be abandoned. The doctors knew that he probably would die if they tried to move him in the ambulance wagons that bumped across rutted fields. Finally it was decided to leave him behind in the care of an orderly.

An old couple in the neighborhood agreed to take the wounded man into their house for money. This was a no-man's-land, where criminals from both armies were roaming in desperation. The orderly, believing that Bedell would certainly die, decided to save his own skin and run away.

The wretched owners of the house took the soldier's food and money and never went near him. For two days and nights Bedell fought for his life, praying for a drink of water. He thought death had come at last when an old black man appeared with a bucket of water.

"Who are you?" asked Bedell, reviving after he had drunk the water.

"A Yankee doctor tried to give me money to check up on you after they left you here, sir," said the old man. "I didn't take the money, but I suspected that these people would cheat you. I am a slave, Dick Runner, and I live on the Van Metre plantation."

That night Dick Runner told Mrs. Van Metre about the abandoned soldier. Betty Van Metre ran as fast as she could to the house, and angrily demanded to see the sick man.

"Why do you care about a Yankee soldier?" they asked.

"I'm a Confederate," declared the young woman, "but I'm not going to see a helpless man die, whatever side he is on. Suppose it were my husband?"

And so began her struggle to save Henry Bedell's life. Dick Runner and Betty took the man to her house where they nursed him. She got medical help, and finally, when she received the message that her own husband was a prisoner, she took Bedell through the battle lines to Washington.

Mrs. Bedell came from Vermont herself to thank the Southern woman, and then they all began a search for Mr. Van Metre, who had become "lost" in a Union hospital.

Both men survived the war, and they and their wives lived for many years, close family friends. Each year the Van Metres visited the Vermont village where the Bedells continued to live, and each year the Bedells returned the visit to the Van Metre plantation in Virginia.

Lucius E. Chittenden wrote a novel about this true story, calling it *An Unknown Heroine,* and copies of the old book can be found on some library shelves today.

The End of the War

When the Civil War was ended in April of 1865, there was hardly a Vermont family not touched with death and poverty. Vermont was almost as devastated as the defeated South.

"What's left for us here?" said many an old farmer as he bitterly realized that he could not carry on the farm work alone with his sons dead or moved away. Often the old couples would get on the train and go West to live with children and grandchildren. Many old farmhouses were silent, and finally their barns caved in with the weight of snow. It almost seemed that the war had defeated Vermont.

8. Who Are the People Who Made Vermont?

What's a Vermonter?

"Grandpa, what's a Vermonter?" asked a Yankee boy a hundred years or more ago.

Grandpa thought a minute. "Why, son, it's a person who chooses to live here and take part in the community," he said. "There's been a lot of talk about 'Vermonters' running the 'foreigners' out, but as I see it, all people were foreigners here once, even the Indians."

"I just wondered," said the boy. "Some fellows at school talk about it. I'll tell them what you said."

"Something about the Green Mountains makes the people who live here get to be a certain way," said the old man thoughtfully. "The people who move here don't change Vermont, but instead they change to Vermonters."

The boy took this thought back to school and became friends with the new Irish and French-Canadian children at recess. When he grew up, the boy married one of his French-Canadian neighbors and together they raised a family of Green Mountain boys and girls.

Scots

After the French people left the shores of Lake Champlain, the first Europeans to make long-lasting settlements in Vermont were descendants of English colonists from Massachusetts and Connecticut. There was only one group who came directly from Europe to settle in Vermont, Scottish people who formed a company in their own country in 1773, and sent an agent to buy land for them.

The agent, James Whitelaw, looked at land in New York and other colonies, but he chose land in the New Hampshire Grants for his friends.

A year later some of the group began to settle the towns of Ryegate and Barnet. When the Revolution broke out in a few years, some of the others were prevented from coming, but in spite of that so many Scots came that Caledonia County was named after the ancient name for Scotland, and Mr. Whitelaw succeeded Ira Allen as Surveyor General for the state of Vermont.

Three Black Men

Vermont had famous black citizens even in the early days. One was Lemuel Haynes, who for thirty years was minister of the Congregational church in West Rutland. He had been adopted by a white family in Massachusetts who had educated the bright little boy well. Like most of the young men of his day, Lemuel Haynes fought in the Revolution, and

LEMUEL HAYNES

there is a legend that he came to Fort Ticonderoga with Benedict Arnold's troops.

The Reverend Mr. Haynes was a handsome and popular preacher, with a sense of humor that made the children of the town love him and tease him. One day some boys joked with him, saying, "Mr. Haynes, did you know that the devil is dead?"

Mr. Haynes raised his hand in a pastoral blessing above the heads of the giggling boys. "You poor fatherless children," he sighed, trying to keep a straight face as he looked heavenward.

Another black man who contributed to Vermont was Alexander Twilight, the first black man in America to earn a college degree when he graduated from Middlebury in 1823. Mr. Twilight founded and was headmaster of Brownington Academy, a famous school in its day. Alexander Twilight was so determined to have a suitable building that he designed and, with only a little help from others, constructed the school building with his own hands. It still stands today in Orleans. No longer a school, it is used to house the Orleans County Historical Society, a reminder of what one man can do if he has the will. Mr. Twilight was the first black state legislator in America when he was elected to the Vermont Assembly in 1836.

George Washington Henderson, who graduated from the University of Vermont in 1877 at the top of his class, was the second black to become a member of Phi Beta Kappa, a national honor society of high-ranking scholars in college. He became a minister, an educator, and a champion of his race.

The mysterious story of how George Henderson came to

Vermont has not been completely established, but a small notice in the *Addison County Journal* of August 1, 1878, says that a "Captain" Carpenter of Waterville had brought home an illiterate former slave, a fourteen-year-old boy named Henderson, and that this boy had become an honor graduate of the University.

Sergeant Zephaniah Carpenter of Waterville, a member of the Eighth Regiment, Company A, of the Vermont Brigade, may be the kind man who brought the possibly lost and orphaned boy from Virginia when he returned to Vermont after serving in the Civil War. Probably the townspeople pitched in to help the youngster to learn, and eventually to enter the University of Vermont.

When Mr. Henderson died in 1936 the secret of his childhood had still not been recorded by the University authorities, but there was no secret about his brilliant college record and his useful life. Among other things, he was principal of Jericho Academy, Craftsbury Academy, and the Newport Graded School. He was a Congregational minister in New Orleans, a dean at Fisk University, and finally a professor of Greek and Latin and Ancient Literature at Wilberforce University in Ohio.

During the years he taught school, he found time to earn a Master of Arts degree from the University of Vermont, at which time he read a paper on "Conservation," a subject not much talked about in those days. He earned another degree at Yale and yet another at the University of Berlin as well as receiving an honorary degree at the University of Vermont.

Franco-Americans

Travelers in northern Vermont who see road signs in French are sometimes surprised. Although Vermont's first French settlers departed centuries ago, the French people in Canada have been close to Vermonters since the state's earliest days, co-operating in smuggling, political struggles, trade, and other projects, for good or evil. Soon after the Revolution some French people came to northern Vermont to farm, and the French language was in Vermont air from the start.

But when railroad construction began in Vermont, the bosses needed more laborers than Vermont could muster.

"Canada has lots of available workers. Let's employ some of the French-Canadians," they said. "We could get them quickly, for they are near by."

French-Canadians who were dissatisfied with Canadian politics and social conditions flocked southward over the border, eager to earn the good wages paid by the railroad companies. Some men went to work on farms, and many of the women found they could get jobs helping out in homes. Soon a number of the French-Canadian families had earned and saved enough money to buy farms of their own in Vermont, where it was easier for a family to get ahead.

By 1850 there were fourteen thousand former French-Canadians living in Vermont, bringing newspapers, churches, and special customs to add zest to the state.

Since the newcomers were almost entirely Catholic, the religious pattern of Vermont changed quickly, especially when the French were joined by the Irish people who also came in great numbers. In 1853 Vermont got its first Catholic bishop, Bishop Louis de Goesbriand, a native of France, who made a mark on the state by setting up orphanages, schools, and a hospital in Burlington that bears his name.

The new bishop soon brought French-speaking priests from Canada to work among the new Vermonters. By 1900 there were fifty-five thousand Franco-Americans in Vermont. So many Vermont families have French ancestors that it is guessed that one in every seven persons in Vermont is related one way or another to the French people of Canada.

The Irish in Vermont

Who would have thought that the potato crop in Ireland would have a tremendous influence on Vermont?

When in 1846 a disease began to destroy the potato crop in Ireland many Irish people who had to live on a potato diet faced starvation. At the same time so many restless Vermonters were moving West that there were not enough men left to fill the jobs on the railroads.

When railroad companies advertised for workers, Irish people who were hungry and dissatisfied with their government poured into the ports of New York, Boston, and Montreal, many of them finding their way to Vermont, joining Irish who had come in the previous decade.

"Patrick, we should go to America," said many an Irish mother, looking at her large brood of hungry children. "There's work to be had in Vermont, which must be a green place like our Emerald Isle."

By 1850 there were fifteen thousand Irish people living in Vermont. Some even came on foot from Montreal with their possessions on their backs like the first settlers from Connecticut.

"The Know-Nothings"

All the people in the state did not welcome the flood of poor immigrants who crowded in day after day, eager for work. Some citizens were afraid they would have to pay higher taxes for schools, and some felt that as soon as the new-comers became naturalized and could vote that they would change the old customs of Vermont. Some feared the number of Catholic immigrants would challenge the established Congregational Church of traditional Yankees.

A few years before the Civil War a secret political party who called themselves the Know-Nothings sprang up in America for the purpose of keeping out foreigners and Catholics.

"Whoa!" said thoughtful Vermonters when the party spread into their state. "Our ancestors came here because they were poor and wanted to build a new life. It's not right for us to exclude the new people."

So many citizens wrote letters to Vermont's many newspapers criticizing this secret party, and so many editors defended the rights of the immigrants, that soon the Know-Nothing party was shamed out of existence in the state.

There were many churches left vacant when Vermonters moved West, and the new Catholic population bought the buildings. Foreign-born fathers became citizens and voted on issues, just as their neighbors did, and children got acquainted at school.

In a few years they were all Vermonters, just as the boy's grandfather had predicted—just ordinary people concerned with the weather and the crops and the economy, whether their names were Smith, O'Riley, Barbatelli, or Rousseau. When the Civil War came, the sons of the new citizens enlisted along with the descendants of the first pioneers, all Americans together.

The Fenian Problems

After the Civil War was over, many Irish-Americans, who belonged to an Irish society called the Fenians, wanted to go after the British in Canada, because most of the immigrants opposed British government in Ireland.

At this moment Americans, especially Vermonters, were annoyed at the Canadian government, for the St. Albans Raid was still fresh in their minds. When the Fenians massed in Vermont in June of 1866 to attack Canada, Vermonters did not stop them.

Fourteen hundred Fenians, mostly from New York and Boston, rode the trains to St. Albans, Swanton, Highgate, and Fairfield. Anyone could have told that this was no summer picnic, but Vermonters kept still. When the Department of State in Washington got wind of the affair, troops were dispatched in a hurry to keep the international boundary neutral.

The Fenians crossed the border anyhow and seized a British flag at the customs house and stirred up a bit of excitement. One Fenian was killed. The Fenians soon were out of ammunition, and the British regulars were advancing, so they withdrew to Vermont. There they signed a parole, and the people of St. Albans had a gay party for the soldiers.

The Fenians tried it again a few years later, and the Canadians fought off the invaders. But when the Fenians retreated to Vermont in 1870 they were arrested. After this both countries put soldiers in the area to keep peace on the border, and the Fenians went home to dream of a lost cause.

Swedes and Finns

"What are we going to do about all these abandoned farms?" asked Alonzo Valentine, a Civil War veteran of Bennington, looking at the idle farms around him. Authorities in Montpelier, worried that one in ten of Vermont's farms was vacant, asked Mr. Valentine if he could try to solve the problem.

He had traveled in the West and had seen the good farms of the Swedish immigrants there. Why not import Swedish farmers to Vermont? Alonzo Valentine wondered.

He drew a map of Vermont showing where the deserted farms were located and printed information about Vermont in Swedish and sent it to Sweden. When twenty-seven Swedish families asked to come, Valentine set up committees to help the newcomers when they arrived in 1890 in Weston, Wilmington, and Vershire, where many of their descendants live today.

Finnish people came to Vermont, too, to work for logging companies and to farm the idle land. Finn Hill in the town of Andover is named for the farmers from Finland who became new settlers in Vermont in the days after the end of the 19th Century.

The farmers may have found the rocks a back-breaking nuisance, but some rocks had a surprising result.

Slate Brings the Welsh

From the earliest days of Vermont, hand-quarried slate was used for roofs and hearths and tombstones, and even for school slates, but after the Civil War the slate mining became so important that slate workers from Wales were brought here.

"The Welsh people are mighty singers," said the local people as the Joneses, the Lloyds, and the Llewelleyens piled into the towns in the slate district west of the Green Mountains, and especially into Poultney. In 1877 alone, one hundred fifty Welsh people came to Vermont, joining friends and relatives already there. People from Wales continued to come to Vermont, and today Welsh names are on mailboxes all over the state.

Granite and the Vermont Italians

When Vermont's State House was built in 1833, Barre granite, great blocks of it, had to be hauled by ox teams to Montpelier. As Barre's granite became famous for monuments and public buildings, experienced workers were needed, and two decades after the close of the Civil War skilled craftsmen began to come from northern Italy. Some Italians had come from southern Italy to work on the railroads in earlier years, but it was Barre that gave Vermont a real Italian town.

Italian food, songs, festivals, and gaiety turned Barre into "Little Italy." Mari Tomasi, one of Vermont's favorite writers, was a Barre girl whose Italian parents owned a grocery store in Montpelier. She wrote of being a little girl peeping over the counter, listening to the tall tales of the stonecutters who came to the Tomasi store to buy cheese and wine and sausage and spaghetti.

"Little girls of four or five years old wore gold earrings in their pierced ears," she recalled. "The immigrants made gardens of their tiny lawns, planting Italian chicory and pungent herbs oftentimes beside a sturdy Vermont maple tree; . . . and so the Old World culture and the Vermont culture began to mingle. The fences enclosing the gardens were covered with grape vines. In the fall of the year neighbor helped neighbor crush the grapes and make the sour Italian wine that was part of their daily meals."

Marble and the Vermont "United Nations"

It was the marble industry of Proctor that brought a real "United Nations" to Vermont. Like granite, marble was used in a limited way for hearths and tombstones in the early days, but after the Civil War when railroads could transport the heavy stone and inventors found better methods of quarrying marble there was a need for experienced stone workers as the industry grew.

For over a hundred years workers of many nationalities have worked with Vermont marble to be used in public buildings all over the world. The Vermont Marble Company in Proctor encouraged European workers to come, until in 1916 there were twenty-three nationalities represented in the town of Proctor. Scandinavians, Spanish, Polish, Greek, German, Russian, English, and Italian children played games and exchanged ideas in the little town with its marble sidewalks.

Miss Emily Proctor, whose family owned the marble quarries, knew that all children need books they feel at home with, and she knew that English was a language still strange to many of the young people in the town.

Why not get children's books in as many languages as there were nationalities in the town, and put them in the town library for all the children to read? Miss Proctor set out

to find the books, and here in this little library in a small
Vermont town grew one of America's most unusual collections of books for young people, and these books are still in
the Proctor Free Library.

She gave adult books in many languages, too, and in the
library people would meet for Polish Day or Italian Day or
Spanish Day to learn folk songs and sample new foods from
other countries—and borrow from the library books in a
familiar language.

Jews in Vermont

Among the newcomers at Proctor and in other parts of the
state were Jews from many countries. Jews had felt welcome
in Vermont since the first Jewish peddlers found this a
friendly place to be. Jews were among the early landholders
in Vermont, and in Poultney there is an old Jewish cemetery
whose headstones tell a long history of Jewish Vermonters.

By 1875 there was a small Jewish congregation in Burlington where the heads of ten families prayed together and
celebrated the holy days of Yom Kippur, Rosh Hashanah,
and the Passover.

Today there are many Jewish congregations in Vermont.

Poles and Spaniards

Polish people came to work in the paper mills at Bellows
Falls, and their relatives, hearing of opportunities in America, came to farm near by.

"I think I'll just go for fun," said teenage Polish girls, hearing of opportunities for jobs in America. A girl might work in
the mills a few years and then marry a Polish boy who had

probably come for adventure, too. In the early 1900's there were more than five hundred new Polish people in Windsor County, and there were others scattered throughout the state.

Spanish people came to work in the granite industry as well as in the marble quarries. They established Spanish clubs and bought homes and businesses and sent back letters to tell their relatives what a good place Vermont was. Many Spanish people settled in Montpelier, where their names are familiar today.

And New Faces Keep Coming

"Now who could those people be?" the residents of Stowe asked each other one summer day in 1942 when two carloads of people, mostly young, with musical instruments and luggage, drove into the town, singing. The newcomers spoke English with a heavy accent and wore traditional Austrian peasant clothes.

"Could they be German spies?" someone asked in alarm, for these were the early years of World War II.

Before long the word went around that the singing group was the Trapp family, who had come to live on an old farm near the town.

People who have seen the play or the movie *The Sound of Music* know something of the family of Baron and Baroness von Trapp of Austria who escaped Hitler's Europe to come to America. They were a musical family, and they made their living singing in concerts.

When finally the Trapp family with their ten children decided to make their home in Vermont, they experienced poverty and hardships on their mountain farm like those of the first pioneers. The family worked hard, however, and their music camps and concerts brought people to Vermont for music and folk dancing year after year.

Today some of the Trapp family are still in Vermont, deeply involved with the sport of cross-country skiing.

Political problems in other countries brought other Europeans to Vermont after World War II. In 1957, when one hundred and one Hungarian political refugees were given scholarships at St. Michael's College, Vermonters turned out to welcome them to town meetings, to the legislature, and to private homes.

The Experiment in International Living, whose world headquarters is in Brattleboro, for many years has set up exchanges between young Americans and young foreigners to visit each other's countries and homes, and to learn new languages and customs. Many Peace Corps workers have been trained at the School for International Training, which is run by the Experiment in Brattleboro.

And then the ski industry has brought German, Swiss, French, Italian, Scandinavian, and Austrian experts to Vermont, setting a fashion for ski chalets, yodeling, and Alpine clothing.

In 1970, almost 82,000 of Vermont's 444,000 population were foreign-born or had foreign parents—about one in every five persons. That does not count the grandchildren and the great-grandchildren of the foreign nationals who have come to Vermont in the past century and a half.

If you are a Vermonter, the chances are that you are a "United Nations" Yankee yourself!

9. Life, People, and Politics after the Civil War

A Few Luxuries

> **THE CLIMAX ATTAINED!!!**
> Estey and Co.'s
> Cottage Organ
> Triumphant!!

This was an advertisement in a Vermont newspaper in 1867. By the time the Civil War was over, Vermonters were ready for some joy in their lives, and Jacob Estey and his organs could provide it. Jacob Estey had been a poor boy who ran away from foster parents and learned the plumbing trade, which in those days meant making and installing lead pipes and copper pumps.

When he was barely past his teens, Jacob came to Brattleboro to work in his trade, but when he began to get orders for lead pipes from organ-makers he decided to make some melodeons, or organs, himself. He loaded them on the back of a wagon, and with a boy to play a tune—for Mr. Estey did not know a note of music—he traveled through Vermont and into New York and Canada and New Hampshire, stopping at farmhouses to show them. Estey sold so many organs that he built a thriving factory, which made his name, his town, and his state famous for music.

There were lace curtains and fancy wallpaper and gas lights in some parlors, and the stores carried more and more ready-made clothes. Private schools and academies sprang up in towns of any size, and farm machinery such as reapers and cream separators made life easier for farmers. Evaporators for making maple syrup replaced the old method of boiling sap in the family potash kettle.

Peddlers came with tempting wares in carts jammed with calico, pots, pans, pins, and kerosene lamps. With railroads and better turnpikes came other kinds of travelers, such as portrait-painters, photographers, dentists, doctors—and a few scoundrels who bedazzled housewives into buying shoddy trinkets. Old Vermont cookbooks show that fish peddlers came selling oysters and clams to Green Mountain farmers, far away from salt water. There were even ice cream freezers advertised in the newspapers!

Medicine shows traveled from town to town with an Indian or a banjo player, or some sort of attraction like a trained animal to catch the attention of people in a village, and then a high-pressure salesman would make wild claims for his remedy. Often the bottle contained little more than sugar and water, but the seller would declare that it would cure everything from measles to falling hair.

Happiness, Holidays, and a Special Birthday

One day a cart with great rolls of paper and pots of paste stopped at a farmhouse near St. Johnsbury. Curious little boys and girls ran to the road to see what kind of peddler was coming now.

"Tell your pa we want to paste circus signs on the side of his barn in exchange for a free ticket," said the man.

Pa, coming in from the field, looked at his big bare barnside. "Well, I might as well. But we want tickets for every one of us."

When the circus parade went down the streets of the town with an elephant, everybody gasped.

"It's Jumbo! It's really Jumbo!" screamed the children as the thirteen-thousand-pound elephant lumbered down the street. Later with ringside seats at the circus, life had never seemed so good!

Gypsies came, too, scaring children who had been warned of being kidnapped by these caravan people. Fathers locked up their barns against horse thieves, but some boys envied the carefree gypsies who had no daily grind of chores in the same old barn, or the same old lessons in the same old schoolhouse.

In the winter there were sleds and toboggans and skates for the lucky ones. Some boys made skooters, or "jack-jumpers," with a barrel stave and a seat where a skillful rider could balance and control as he tore down the hill. Boys made kites and whistles and girls did fancy handwork, and everybody had fun at the "bees" where people got together for husking, quilting, apple-paring, and gathering wild berries. There were picnics, square dances, singing schools, barn-raisings, and sugar-on-snow parties in the spring.

In Springfield, inventor Joel Ellis added a line of doll

carriages and jointed dolls to the things made in his factory. The Ellis dolls were durable, with maple-wood heads and bodies, jointed so that they could kneel to say their prayers, bend to stand on their heads, or put their hands behind them.

At Christmastime village stores had wax and china dolls, metal candle-holders for Christmas trees, and tops and toy trains, as well as lemon drops, candy sticks, ribbon candy, and sleds with metal runners.

"Christmas is a newfangled notion," grumbled old folks who had grown up in the Puritan traditions that did not believe in celebrating Christmas.

But everybody agreed on Thanksgiving with its feast and a family gathering; and there was even time for a bit of fun at Halloween when the town "toughies" might turn over an outhouse or two.

The Fourth of July was a noisy holiday with cannons shooting, fireworks blazing and popping, and patriotic speeches and toasts by the hour. Some towns raised money for band instruments so that a marching band could lead the town parade. Calvin Coolidge, who was later to become President of the United States, was born in Plymouth on the Fourth of July in 1872.

Today his childhood house is a memorial where visitors can go to see how Vermonters lived more than a century ago. Calvin and his sister made quilts or whittled bits of wood by the fire in the evening, for even little children's hands were never idle.

Several years before Calvin was born, the villages at Plymouth Notch and at Plymouth Center got together to buy a cannon so they could be sure of a big boom on the Glorious Fourth, but who was to keep the cannon? One of Calvin's relatives was chosen to store it in his barn in Plymouth Notch.

"Why should the Notch get to bring out the cannon and do the shooting?" said the young men of the other village who wanted to keep the prized cannon in their settlement. So, every year with a lot of muffled laughter and horseplay, the men would try to steal the cannon, and if they succeeded, the men from the Notch tried to steal it back.

"Who'll win this year?" wondered the little boy as he watched the sun come up on his birthday, which would be celebrated with more excitement than any day in the year.

The Grange

At the end of the Civil War the United States was bitterly divided and many farms in both the North and South were neglected or damaged.

"We must get our farmers to unite to restore our country's land," said thoughtful people in the Bureau of Agriculture in Washington. "It's time to put war behind us and look to the future."

So an organization was formed for all Americans to bring back the farms. It was called the Patrons of Husbandry, and had local clubs called "Granges."

Jonathan Lawrence of St. Johnsbury loved the Vermont land. His mother, Deborah Ide, had walked to Vermont from Massachusetts leading a cow when she was only fifteen years old, in 1790, and he knew how hard people had worked to build farms, and how important it was to keep them going. Why not organize a Grange in Vermont to help farmers?

"Women can join, too," said the Grange organizers, and

the women flocked to become members. Soon local Granges were all over the state, forming co-operatives to help farmers buy work-saving machines and cheaper and better supplies. The Grange helped farmers to sell their products at better prices, and the Grange halls became centers of social life in many towns, where members could gather for a community supper and fill up on baked beans and apple pie.

Senator Justin Smith Morrill

Senator Justin Smith Morrill of Strafford was another of Vermont's men who helped his state after the Civil War. When Justin was fourteen years old and a bright student at Thetford Academy, he wanted to go to college more than anything in the world. But his family was poor and large, with Justin the eldest of ten children.

"Son, if I take all my money and send you to college, what will happen to the education of the rest of the family?" asked his father.

"You should divide among us all equally, Father," said young Justin slowly, realizing how unfair it would be for him to have advantages at the expense of the younger ones.

SEN. JUSTIN MORRILL

So the boy went to work as a clerk in the general store of the town. Thirty years later he owned the store and had ample money in the bank, but he had not stopped studying even though he had stopped school. He had made up his own course of study and read law and architecture and classic literature and history, so that he was an educated leader when a chance came for him to run for public office when he was forty-five years old. Justin Morrill was elected to Congress, and for forty-four years before, during, and after the Civil War he served in the United States House of Representatives and in the Senate.

Senator Morrill was responsible for many of Washington's monuments and buildings, but he is most remembered as the man who made college education possible for many more people. Remembering the disappointment of his boyhood ambition to go to college, he worked to persuade the President and the Congress to pass a law to grant public lands to states for universities to "promote the liberal and practical education of the industrial classes."

In 1862 the Morrill Act was passed which created "land-grant" colleges.

Today men and women who can go to agricultural colleges and state universities owe a debt to the boy who educated himself so that his younger brothers and sisters could have an equal chance, making higher education possible for future generations.

PRESIDENT
CHESTER
ARTHUR

President Chester Arthur

During the years that Justin Morrill was in the Senate, a fellow Vermonter was President. Chester Arthur, who was believed to be born in Fairfield where his father was a Baptist minister, was elected Vice President in 1880. When President Garfield was assassinated less than a year later, Arthur became President.

America was in a state of great political unrest in the years that Arthur was President. He had many enemies and he was not elected to serve the next term. President Arthur was considered America's handsomest President, and he is said to have owned sixty-seven suits of clothes and thirty-four extra pairs of trousers when he was in the White House!

George Perkins Marsh, Conservationist

When eight-year-old George Perkins Marsh of Woodstock developed an eye disease in 1809 that kept him from reading, life seemed bleak indeed.

"What will I do?" George asked himself sadly. No school, no storybooks, nothing to do—maybe for as long as a few years, the doctor had said.

George was too bright to mope for long. "If I can't read, then I'll go outside and observe the world and train my mind to remember as much as it can hold," he determined.

George rambled in the woods and fields summer and winter, watching nature at work and thinking about the effect of people on their environment.

"The bubbling brook, the trees, the flowers, the wild animals were to me persons, not things," he said later in life, adding that he felt that even trees had personality.

When George Marsh grew up he was famous and beloved as a scholar, statesman, and naturalist. He helped found the Smithsonian Institution in Washington when he was representing Vermont in Congress. Later he became Ambassador to Italy, and in his travels he kept right on following his boyhood habit of observing the natural world. He saw how man had destroyed nature in Europe, and he wanted to teach Americans to take care of their country.

In 1864 he published a book called *Man and Nature*, telling of man's effect on the natural world. Not only Vermonters but people everywhere read and thought about Marsh's book, which pointed out that land was precious and that man had an obligation to take care of it. He knew that even in Vermont, hillsides had been eroded by poor farming practice and by careless cutting and burning of forests.

George Perkins Marsh was one of the first conservationists, and his book is influencing the world today.

Carrie Burnham Kilgore, Lawyer

The women who had served as nurses or run farms and businesses while their husbands were away on the battlefields did not go meekly back to their old ways when the Civil War ended. One of them was Carrie Burnham of Craftsbury, an orphan girl who had worked to get herself a high-school education.

Supporting herself as a teacher, she was able at the same time to study physiology and physical education, both of which were new fields for women in those days. She worked as a doctor's assistant and a teacher and introduced gymnastics for girls in Philadelphia, all the while becoming more aware of the legal problems of women.

"I'll become a lawyer," she declared. Although no law school would accept her, she studied with a lawyer who believed in her.

In 1871, law-student Carrie Burnham registered as a voter and paid her poll tax in Philadelphia, but voting officials tore up her ballot because women were not allowed to vote.

"I'll take it to court," she declared. But she lost the case.

In the meantime Carrie Burnham married lawyer Damon Kilgore and had two daughters. Still denied admission to law school, she was not allowed to take the bar examinations. In 1881 Carrie Kilgore was finally admitted to the University of Pennsylvania Law School, and two years later she became its first woman graduate and was admitted to practice.

She never stopped doing new things. When she was seventy years old Carrie Kilgore went up in a balloon! She died a year later, and is buried in Craftsbury.

Abby Hemenway, Historian and Editor

In Ludlow an energetic young woman took on a giant-size cause: she wanted to write down everything—yes, everything—about Vermont.

It began when this ambitious school teacher filled her spare time gathering newspaper poems by Vermonters and brought them out in a book just on the eve of the Civil War. When the public liked the book, Miss Hemenway decided she would rather gather information than teach school.

"I'll find a reliable person in every town in Vermont, and have him write down everything he can find about his town. Then if these stories can all be bound together in a set of books, that will be almost everything there is to be known about Vermont," she reasoned.

She began with Addison County in spite of all sorts of discouraging predictions from the leading men of Middlebury who didn't believe a young woman could possibly produce such a history. True, Abby Hemenway was not very good at business, but she got things rolling at once. By 1860 the first volume was published. For the next thirty years, in spite of fires and financial failure, she kept on. Debt drove her out of Vermont. She had no money to pay a printer so she learned to set type herself.

When she died in 1890 she had published four volumes, the fifth was three-fourths finished—to be finished by her sister the following year—and the sixth, on Windsor County, was not done. Today Abby Hemenway's *Gazetteer*, its enormous volumes packed with warm details of early Vermont, are guarded treasures in Vermont's libraries.

More Busy Women

In 1870, a year when changes in Vermont's Constitution were being considered, some Vermont men thought it was time to pass a law for women to vote. Famous women's-rights speakers came to Vermont to help the cause.

Crowds came to Montpelier to hear speeches by Lucy Stone, Mary Livermore, Julia Ward Howe, and William Lloyd Garrison. One of the railroads gave passes to women, who came by the hundreds. In many towns women met and signed petitions.

"Mother, are you willing to sign this petition for a law to allow women to vote in elections?" a young woman in St. Johnsbury asked her mother when the paper circulated through the town.

"Of course I'll sign," answered the mother, reaching for a pen. "I've been hoping for something like this since Clarina Nichols stirred up the Vermont women thirty years ago."

In spite of all the publicity the legislation did not pass.

However, in 1875 two women were graduated from the University of Vermont, and in 1880 a law was finally passed permitting Vermont women to vote in district school meetings and hold office in local school systems.

Annie Ide and Her Perfectly Marvelous Present

When Judge Henry Ide of St. Johnsbury was appointed American Governor of Samoa, one of his neighbors in his new post was Robert Louis Stevenson, whose books *Kidnapped* and *Treasure Island* had delighted many Vermont young people.

When gentle Mr. Stevenson heard that little Annie Ide,

who was still at home in St. Johnsbury, had written her father that she was sad because her birthday fell on Christmas, Mr. Stevenson decided he must do something about it.

"Tut," he said, "a child is entitled to have a birthday and Christmas as well, not both rolled into one."

So Robert Louis Stevenson, who was as imaginative and full of fun as he was gentle and beloved, gave Annie Ide his own birthday!

Today in the Fairbanks Museum in St. Johnsbury there lies in a glass case near the doll collection a legal document dated 1891, part of which says—

> "In consideration that Miss Annie H. Ide . . . was born out of all reason, upon Christmas Day, and is therefore out of all justice denied the consolation and profit of a proper birthday;
>
> And, considering that I, the said Robert Louis Stevenson, have attained an age when, oh, we never mention it, and that I have now no further use for a birthday of any description:
>
> . . . do hereby transfer to Annie Ide all and whole my right and privileges in the thirteenth day of November, formerly my birthday, and hereby and henceforth the birthday of Annie H. Ide, to have, hold, exercise, and enjoy the same in the customary manner, by the sporting of fine raiment, eating of rich meats and receipt of gifts, compliments, and copies of verse, according to the manner of our ancestors . . ."

So on November 13th Annie Ide put on her white dress with the blue sash and celebrated her perfectly marvelous present of a new birthday.

Mr. Kipling in Vermont

RUDYARD
KIPLING

The story of Annie Ide's birthday appeared in *St. Nicholas,* a famous magazine that children everywhere read for half a century. So did *The Jungle Book* and other tales by Rudyard Kipling which were written in Brattleboro during the 1890's when the author lived there.

When Kipling's whale in *The Just So Stories* opened his mouth "wide and wide and wide and said 'Change here for Winchester, Ashuelot, Nashua, Keene, and stations on the Fitchburg Road,'" Mr. Kipling was calling the stations on a Vermont-bound railroad!

Rudyard Kipling was a world-famous writer, and autograph seekers who came to Brattleboro annoyed him no end. Kipling, who always loved children, hit upon a plan that pleased everybody.

"If you want my autograph," he said, "you must pay two dollars to the fresh air fund that brings poor city children to Vermont for a summer holiday."

Nobody knows how many young people benefited from Kipling's "fresh air autographs," but fresh air children have continued to visit the Green Mountains to this day.

Mrs. McKinley's Butter

Politics have been the spice of life to Vermonters from the early conventions up until today. Town Meeting tempers have often been hot, but in 1896 some fun crept into the political picture that filled the newspapers for weeks.

Ohio's Governor William McKinley, a great favorite in Vermont, was running for President in 1896. In September some Vermont boosters decided that it would be exciting to

run a special train all the way to Ohio to congratulate him
on his nomination.

A hundred merrymaking passengers boarded a fourteen-
car special train decorated with banners and pictures of
McKinley. They took along a band and a glee club, and
every man had a flag and a handsome badge.

Of course, they wanted to take a gift to the man who later
became President, so they attached a special refrigerator
car, a Vermont invention, to the train and carried in it a nine-
foot cross made of golden Vermont butter. This was a symbol of the "gold standard" of McKinley's platform, a policy
of which Vermont voters approved.

When the train got to Ohio all the Vermonters walked in a
parade to the McKinley home, carrying the buttery cross.
What do you suppose Mrs. McKinley did with all that butter? Made cookies?

Admiral George Dewey

ADMIRAL
GEORGE
DEWEY

In 1898 the Spanish-American War stirred the country.
When Vermont's admiral George Dewey, who was in charge
of the Asiatic fleet in Hong Kong harbor, moved his ships to
Manila in the Philippines and defeated the Spanish fleet,
Vermont went wild with enthusiasm for her favorite son.
George Dewey as a boy in Montpelier had played ball on the
State House lawn and had walked backward down the gran-
ite steps with his eyes shut. This was a favorite sport in those
days when girls wore button-up shoes and the boys wore
copper-toed boots.

Vermont could hardly do enough to honor the naval hero.
Special trains took him to major towns, where horse-drawn
carriages paraded him through streets lined with cheering

people who waved flags and threw flowers in his path. There were bands and bunting from one end of the state to the other, reminding some old people of the celebrations for Lafayette less than a century before. But what a century it had been!

The End of the Century

But in the long run, the most recent heroes were not as important to Vermont as cows. The first settlers came leading a cow, if they had one, and by the time Vermont was a hundred years old purebred cattle had multiplied in Vermont's pastures until her milk, butter, and cheese were famous. There was an average of twelve cows to a farm, to make a total almost as great as the number of people in the whole state.

Summer visitors brought revenue to the state, too. Mining, making maple sugar, growing grain and other crops; and small industries, including paper, woolens, printing, and publishing, kept Vermont prosperous.

Powerhouses with generators were being built along Vermont streams, and on the eve of the new century forty Vermont towns had electric lights. There were a few telephones, St. Johnsbury having put in the first one in 1877. Gas lights had been used in some towns for half a century. There were even electric streetcars to replace the old horse-drawn trolley cars in the larger towns.

When the 1800's came to an end at the last midnight of 1899, with church bells ringing and fireworks blazing and train whistles blowing, Vermont was ready for the new century.

10. Vermont
in the 20th Century

Through World War I

Molly Robinson, Being a Vermont Girl

What was it like, being a girl in Vermont in 1900? At Rowland Robinson's home, "Rokeby," in Ferrisburg, is a diary written by fifteen-year-old Molly Robinson who told about what she wore and ate and did and thought.

The Robinson family had little money, but they were far better off than the average Vermont family of the day for they were well educated and important people, who had contributed their talents to the state since its early days.

Although her family were Quakers, Molly preferred the lively doings at the Congregational Church, where bad boys hid the food at Sunday School picnics, and the young people put on plays they called "farces."

Molly and her friends made valentines from pink-and-white paper for friends at school. Giggling, they made a special one with a picture of a pair of false teeth pasted on it, and gave it to their teacher at Vergennes High School, who was "sweet on" the town dentist. Molly's sister Rachael bought her a suit and a straw hat in Burlington "at the fire sale."

Molly and her friends organized a secret society with secret names for each other, and they wore baby-blue ribbon bows as the club's symbol.

There were fireworks on the Fourth of July and on Election Day.

Molly had a bicycle, and a camera, and she gave and received a lot of Christmas presents which she carefully listed. She rode a horse around the farm, and reported that her high school class went camping overnight.

Peddlers were still coming to Vermont farmhouses in 1900. One who visited Molly's family was an Italian scissors-grinder who sharpened all the knives and scissors in the house in exchange for spending the night. He told a wide-eyed Molly about life in Italy.

A washerwoman named Cora came weekly to do the family wash by hand in big washtubs.

Many families had sleighs, and one evening twenty-seven young people went sleigh-riding behind a huffing team of horses with "seven strings of bells and two horns." Molly stayed out until after midnight, singing, laughing, keeping warm with fur robes and crowded bodies.

One evening Molly took her guitar and songbook to the Christian Endeavor meeting for the hymn-singing, which lasted for an hour. They had ice cream and cake for refreshments, but "there was not enough of either." They played games such as "Quack" and "Bird, Beast, and Fish."

But life was not all happy for Molly Robinson. She worried that she couldn't get along better with her mother who, Molly felt, did not understand her. She was impatient with her father, who was very sick, and she was ashamed

that she was a little bit envious of her beautiful older sister Rachael, an artist who had lots of beaux. Molly wished boys would pay more attention to her and ask her to go riding as often as they asked Rachael.

When Molly finally had to drop out of school to help nurse her father, she sometimes stayed by his side all night to let her mother sleep. She read to her father, and some days her blind father dictated stories, for he was busy finishing a new book despite his illness.

Usually Molly was up at six o'clock in the morning and worked very hard house-cleaning and helping about the farm with its twenty-two cows and eight pigs. Molly wrote that she detested feeding the chickens.

"I don't like hens. Ours have been troubled so much with lice that when I go after the eggs I get all covered with them which isn't very pleasant."

Molly listed the fifty-seven books she owned, which included Miss Alcott's books and *Black Beauty*. At the end of the year her father died and Molly went away to school, never making any more entries in her diary, for when she came home again she felt too grown up for girlish diary-keeping.

Automobiles

Molly Robinson doesn't mention in her diary the new marvel that everybody was talking about at the turn of the century: automobiles.

In 1900 most people had never heard of the fact that, about sixty-five years before, inventor John Gore of Halifax and Brattleboro had built a steam-buggy that went all the way to Massachusetts at 10 to 15 miles an hour, belching sparks from the fire that kept the boilers going to make the steam to propel it. Gore's steam-wagon scared the horses and people so much that he was forbidden to put it on the roads, and he moved away.

The citizens of Barre were agog in 1900 when W. A. Lane built a steam-wagon that could carry a two-ton load up a hill with no horses to pull it.

But it was the new gasoline buggies that caught the fancy of the people. In 1905 there were two hundred seventy automobiles in the state, enough so that the owners had organized an automobile club. With nearly fifteen thousand miles of bumpy Vermont roads for automobiles to explore, the horseless carriages went everywhere, terrifying horses, and people, too.

Daring riders in dusters and veils sat on high seats while people rushed out to see the new contraptions roar by at 5 miles an hour. People talked endlessly about them.

"They won't last. They're just a fad," some people dismissed the noisy, dust-making monsters.

"They'll have to use them only on certain roads," said others. Selectmen set speed limits, and the state required owners to buy a license that cost two dollars.

Newspapers promoted toy autos for Christmas stockings, "to meet the craze for motor cars," as one advertisement said.

Out in California, where he was visiting in 1903, Burlington's Dr. H. Nelson Jackson sat arguing about cars with some companions.

"I tell you, one of these days a car will be driven from coast to coast," said Dr. Jackson. "Why, even I could do it."

"I bet you fifty dollars you can't," retorted a friend.

Dr. Jackson was a man to take a dare.

"Done!" he agreed, committing himself to the long drive home, an unheard-of feat.

Dr. Jackson found a young mechanic, Sewall Crocker, to come with him, and bought a Winton touring car for the expedition. On May 23, 1903, they set out, compass in hand, on a driving trip that was to last more than two months.

They named the car *Vermont* and took along a bulldog named Bud for a mascot. Day after day they forded streams, dug their way out of mud, repaired tires and mechanical parts, and clung to narrow roads on the sides of mountains. There were no filling stations, no garages, no road maps, no motels. Often there were no bridges or even roads. They met astonished people who had never even heard of an automobile.

Wheels fell off and axles broke, and they mended them with whatever they could find. But they kept on going, carrying their five-gallon cans of gasoline along with them. Newspapers all over America picked up the story of the intrepid "beelists," as they were called, and local reporters telegraphed the progress each time Jackson and Crocker drove the now battered car into a town.

When the *Vermont* and its drivers reached New York City, crowds of newspaper reporters acclaimed the first automobile ride across the northern United States and Dr. Jackson became a celebrity. In a few weeks he drove his car in triumph to his home in Burlington, the winner of the fifty-dollar dare.

Railroads

By 1900 more than a thousand miles of railroads linked Vermont's larger towns with each other and the outer world.

Rutland, St. Albans, Brattleboro, Burlington, and St. Johnsbury were all rail centers, and many small villages had railroad passenger stations with freight and telegraph offices to allow people, goods, and messages to flow in and out.

By later standards much of the local travel was very slow. Even in the 20th Century wood-burning locomotives poked along, stopping here and there to refuel. Sometimes young people got out to play or pick flowers beside the tracks while older passengers helped the crew load wood. Such leisurely travel sometimes only accomplished ten miles an hour, or less.

But the main Vermont railroads on either side of the Green Mountains were important because they served as links with the Canadian lines which fed into Vermont, making the state a corridor for imported goods from the great seaport of Montreal. Eventually the Canadian lines owned many of the Vermont railroads.

Building railroads over the Green Mountains was a difficult engineering feat. By 1900 there were five lines leading from east to west. Marble, granite, talc, and other minerals, as well as manufactured goods and farm products, could now reach the market freely. But in spite of these assets, the railroads did not prosper in the 20th Century, for they constantly changed hands and were often so badly managed that they went bankrupt.

Finally, the lonesome sound of train whistles in the night grew more and more rare as highways with automobiles, buses, and trucks began to expand in the 1920's. The 1927 Flood was the death blow to railroads, for hundreds of miles of tracks were washed out and never replaced.

By the 1960's there was almost no passenger service, and little railroad stations were sold to the highest bidders, who often used them for vacation homes. People helped themselves to metal pieces of track and wooden ties, and weeds overran the railroad beds.

In the 1970's many people realized that the loss of railroads was a blow to the nation, and AMTRAK, a federally financed organization, succeeded in bringing back limited train service, a New York-to-Montreal route with a few stops on the way in Vermont.

Snowflake Bentley

A Vermonter who showed the world a new way to look at snow was Wilson Bentley, a Jericho farm boy born at the end of the Civil War, who invented a way to photograph snowflakes before they melted and to measure raindrops.

"That Bentley child is a strange one, all right," said neighbors, shaking their heads over the shy little boy in the black homespun jacket who liked to stand for hours studying the snowflakes that fell on his sleeve. "He ought to be called 'Snowflake' himself," laughed another.

The name stuck—affectionately, for everybody liked him. The Bentley farm was remote, and "Snowflake" wasn't very strong, so most of his winter days were spent at home where his mother saw to his school lessons and taught him music as well. The family owned an encyclopedia which the youngster read avidly, hoping to find out why all snowflakes had six sides.

"If I had a magnifying glass, I could find out more," he said to his parents. The family was poor, but his father reluctantly bought him a glass that made the snow crystals easier to see. Snowflake soon realized that a microscope was what he needed.

"When I taught school we had a microscope," said his mother. "Maybe I could get it for you."

The microscope opened a new world for the boy. Working outdoors in bitter weather, for of course snowflakes melt very fast, he would select a drop of snow and study it on a glass slide, trying to sketch it quickly while holding a pencil awkwardly in his mittened hand. Never like another, each flake seemed more beautiful than the one before.

The young scientist's method was to catch the snow on a black-painted board which he carried carefully to his cold workshop, with gloves on his hands to keep any body warmth from reaching the delicate crystals. Then with a wooden stick he picked up the snowflake and put it on the slide of the microscope, holding his breath all the while.

"How lovely they are! I need to preserve them somehow so I can study the patterns and share them with other people," he thought, frustrated with his drawing, as he examined the fleeting jewels under his lens. "If only I could photograph them."

Photograph! That would be the answer. There were a few photographers in Vermont, but the youth had never seen a camera. He studied what he could find in the encyclopedia and told his parents about his idea.

"You ought to stick to your music," said his father, grumbling a bit again at his son's new ideas. "You should make your living farming and teaching music."

But his parents were finally sympathetic and bought him a big box camera. For months on end he studied the camera, took it apart, and by trial and error figured out a way to attach the camera to a microscope so that he could photograph a snowflake onto a glass plate, by using just the right lens opening and pointing the camera at the sky.

During a snowstorm on January 15, 1885, when he was

twenty years old, he took the world's first successful photograph of a snowflake. Soon he found out that by careful handwork he could scrape away the background, leaving the enlarged image of the snow crystal on glass, clear and detailed. By 1900 scientists were coming to the Jericho farm to learn from Bentley.

He made thousands upon thousands of photographs of snowflakes. Some of them were sold to jewelers or cloth manufacturers for designs. Most of them were used by universities for teaching science.

Bentley was also the first person to photograph and measure raindrops by letting a drop fall onto a tray of flour. As each raindrop fell into the flour it formed a small pellet of dough the size of the raindrop, which he could then measure.

As he continued his experiments Bentley discovered so many new things about weather predictions, the formation of clouds, and meteorology that he wrote articles for scientific magazines, and gave lectures at universities, all the while continuing to farm and work on experiments with snowflakes, raindrops, and dewdrops.

When he died at the old farmhouse in 1931 his neighbors seemed surprised at how famous he was. They thought of him only as being the kindest man in town, a man who liked to sing with the Jericho children, who called him "Uncle Willie." They knew he was a man who liked to do secret good deeds for the people around him, and that he gave all his spare money—and some he couldn't spare—to the fresh air fund for poor city children. He even had a hobby of taking pictures of smiles which he catalogued as he did his snowflake pictures. But famous? Why, it never crossed the neighbors' minds that Snowflake Bentley was renowned throughout the world.

Outdoors, Winter and Summer

As if motor cars were not enough to stir the Green Mountains, a Brattleboro youth named Fred Harris began to try some ski-jumping on a hill near his home in 1907. Vermont boys had always experimented with sliding down hills on barrel staves or smooth runners. At Dartmouth College, where he had organized the Outing Club, young Harris talked with Europeans who were filled with enthusiasm for a more sophisticated kind of skiing, which they liked to try on some of Vermont's snow-covered mountains.

Fred Harris's passion for skiing infected his friends, and soon better skiing equipment, ski clubs, and winter carnivals appeared in schools and towns. Skiers trudged up hills and raced down, while the more hardy climbed up for daring jumps.

"This climbing uphill is a terrible waste of time," complained weekend visitors who took the train to Woodstock for brief holidays for winter sports. "There must be a better way to get more runs in a day."

"Up in Canada they're pulling skiers uphill mechanically, I heard," said someone.

"Let's all put in some money and see if we can build something like that here," cried another enthusiastically.

By 1933 the first rope tow in the United States—1,800 feet long and driven by a Ford truck motor—was operating at Woodstock. Soon Stowe and Bromley had lifts, and Vermont was attracting skiers from all over the world. Today Vermont's ski industry brings in over fifty million dollars a year.

Cross-country skis and snowshoes take old and young skiers close to nature in the winter woods, and in the 1960's snowmobiling became an important outdoor sport for many thousands of people. Tobogganing, skating, ice-fishing, ice-

boating, sledding, and so on, involve so many people in winter sports that special laws have been passed to protect the winter land to preserve it for future generations to enjoy.

Although Green Mountain people had always loved the outdoors, the interest in winter sports seemed to renew excitement in hiking, mountain climbing, and camping in the summer. James P. Taylor, one of the teachers at Vermont Academy at Saxtons River, encouraged his students to clean up woodland trails so more people could walk in natural surroundings, away from signs of civilization. In 1910, a group of old and young banded together to form the Green Mountain Club and began building the Long Trail so that Vermonters and visitors could walk through the Green Mountains on marked trails from Canada to Massachusetts.

Summer camps for boys and girls became the fashion, and Vermont turned into such a favorite summer place for city tourists that boardinghouses and summer hotels were filled with people who came by train or automobile to ride horseback, swim, and enjoy the country life, bringing prosperity to landlords.

"We must take care of our Green Mountains," said people who were beginning to realize more and more that forests and fields must be cherished if they were to last.

Young People Get Together

Boys in Barre in 1909 were excited about a wonderful idea. William F. Milne had just returned from a visit to Scotland, bringing with him news about an organization for boys that had recently been founded by England's Robert Baden-Powell.

"They're called Boy Scouts," said someone. "The members

are very keen on the outdoors, and they try to learn as many skills as possible in the wilds. Vermont would be a wonderful place for Boy Scouts."

Barre boys listened with interest. It sounded just like the sort of things they liked to do—hiking, studying the outdoors, and camping. So on October 29, 1909, fourteen Barre youths met with Mr. Milne at the First Baptist Church to establish the first Boy Scout Troop in America. One of the charter members, Deane Davis, later became Governor of Vermont. In 1950 a postage stamp was issued in honor of this Vermont "first."

At about the same time, the University of Vermont Agricultural Extension Service wanted to encourage farm children to get together for fun and learning. Some of the Extension Service workers, called County Agents, went on snowshoes or horseback from farm to farm to tell young people what others their age were doing. When in 1914 the federal government set aside some money for a youth organization, the Vermont 4–H Club got its start.

Helped by the Extension Service, young people did everything from sheep-raising to sewing. When they could meet, there were basketball games, sleigh rides, and contests. Soon summer camps for boys and girls were set up, and the 4–H became a part of Vermont life.

In the fall of 1917, Mrs. Clara Cooper of Wilder was teaching a girls' Sunday school class. Young Mrs. Cooper, who had heard about the Girl Scout organization, wanted to start a troop for her class. As there were no Girl Scouts then in Vermont, all she had for help was a Girl Scout *Handbook*.

"My husband was a scoutmaster," she wrote, "so I borrowed ideas from the Boy Scouts for some of the activities. As I was feeling my way in learning about Girl Scouting, I had the first troop for only my group of church school girls.

The program was so interesting and we all enjoyed it so much that the next year I asked a Catholic friend, who had two girls the age of my Scouts, if she would come into the troop as assistant leader. That opened the troop to any girl in the village, and we had a wonderful group of girls."

Girl Scouts thrive in Vermont today, and in 1962 the National Girl Scout Roundup was held at Button Bay on Lake Champlain, with a postage stamp issued to commemorate the event.

Aviation

When eighteen-year-old George Schmitt of Rutland read of men flying in planes he was on fire to try it.

"I bet I can make a glider," he said to his brother Charles in 1909. He did, and flew the machine successfully from a bluff in a meadow near his home. The next year he bought an airplane which he tried to fly at the Rutland Fair. There were problems with the engine, but he finally got the plane off the ground on September 8, 1910. It was a hop of only a few hundred yards, however, and experts did not consider this a real flight.

Meanwhile, teenager Charles Hampson Grant of Peru was dreaming of gliding through the air. All the summer of 1909 he read and studied scientific magazines and experimented with designs, but his first machine failed. Undaunted, he tried again the next year, and with the help of his brother and his best friend he built a glider of muslin, spruce, and picture-wire, and he took his bicycle apart to use the seat and handlebars. Finally, on August 15, 1910, fifteen-year-old Charles rolled it from the roof of his house and guided it in a 70-foot flight to land successfully in the meadow below.

Charles Willard of New York made the first honest-to-goodness airplane flight in Vermont at the Caledonia County Fair in St. Johnsbury on September 15, 1910. The plane came by train from Boston, for early planes were not able to fly such distances. While ten thousand farmers and their families held their breath for the thrill of a lifetime, Willard clutched the steering-wheel in front of his unprotected little seat over the wings, and took off from the race track for a perfect six-minute flight.

"They say he got paid a thousand dollars to do it," said someone in awe.

"I'd have charged a million," said another Vermonter. "It's unnatural for man to fly, just as it's unnatural for men to drive in horseless carriages."

But others felt an excitement they had never known before. Some even shed tears, knowing that man could actually fly.

In 1916, Springfield's James Hartness, who would one day be Governor of Vermont, was granted the first amateur pilot's license in the state. Young Hartness had gone to work in a machine shop when he was sixteen.

"That James is a born inventor," said his co-workers as the young man quickly thought of better ways to do things. James rose to the top of his field as the automobile industry made Springfield's machine shops prosper.

He was fifty-five years old when he decided to learn to fly, and it was through his interest that Springfield opened the first airfield and flying school in Vermont. The greatest flying honor that came to Springfield was on the day that Charles A. Lindbergh landed there on July 27, 1927, and Vermonters could see the famous flyer who had made the first solo flight across the Atlantic Ocean, from New York to Paris.

The age of aviation had arrived.

World War I

For several years before America entered World War I, American soldiers guarded railroads and bridges near the Canadian border in Vermont, for Canada was at war with Germany.

It was cold in the tents, and no doubt the soldiers grumbled about having to guard the points of entry into Vermont. But farmers in the neighborhood took the soldiers under their wings and sent over hot apple pies and cookies to lonesome soldiers who shivered in the winter weather.

When America entered the war in 1917, Vermont's one regiment was prepared. Vermont sent sixteen thousand soldiers, sailors, and aviators, plus nurses, staff helpers, and Red Cross workers. At home, guards kept watch on Vermont's vital war industries to prevent enemy sabotage, and people bought war bonds.

Young people, especially the 4-H Club members, planted victory gardens to help the world food shortage when the Vermont Extension Service asked them to help grow and preserve food. The Vermont Department of Agriculture set up Camp Vail at Lyndon as a training camp where one hundred fifty boys were taught new methods of haying, wood-cutting, and gardening.

"If we don't work hard, they'll send us home," said the boys to each other.

"But if they do keep us, we'll get a farm job and be paid fourteen dollars a week," said someone else. The boys worked hard for the rewards and for patriotic reasons, and for the good times they had. At night they sat around the campfire and sang war songs, and sometimes they made up their own verses. One, to the tune of "Keep the Home Fires Burning," was everybody's favorite. It went this way:

Keep the home soil turning,
Keep the old farm earning,
While our lads are far away,
We'll work at home.

While the Huns they're cracking
They shall have our backing.
Turn the old sod inside out
Till the boys come home.

After the war was over, people in Europe were starving, and Vermonters kept the farms producing for people abroad. Church groups, the Red Cross, patriotic societies, college people—everybody pitched in to help. Dorothy Canfield Fisher, one of Vermont's best-loved writers, followed her husband to France and did war work in Europe.

From the 1920's Through the Great Depression

Women Get the Vote, and More!

As in previous wars, Vermont women had capably stepped in to run things at home while the men were off fighting in World War I. When peace came, the cry for equal voting rights for women finally got action. In 1920 the Nineteenth Amendment was passed by Congress and ratified by enough states to give women citizens the right to vote in all elections.

Miss Edna Beard of Orange became Vermont's first woman legislator when the House of Representatives convened in 1921, and there has not been a session without women since then.

Two decades before, on the very day that Admiral Dewey

had made his triumphant return home from the Spanish American War, a baby girl, Consuelo, was born into the Northrop family in Fairfield.

"Too bad it's not a boy," said one of the men in the neighborhood as they sat exchanging news about the war hero and the happenings of the town.

Little Connie Northrop didn't let being a girl stand in the way. She was just old enough to vote when the Nineteenth Amendment made it possible. Soon she became a lawyer, then a legislator, and by 1953 she was Speaker of the Vermont House of Representatives. Two years later she was elected America's first woman Lieutenant Governor.

In 1953 when Mrs. Bailey was elected Speaker, there were fifty-two Vermont women in the legislature, more than any state had ever had. A national magazine came and took a picture of Vermont's distinguished woman lawmakers, and people everywhere took notice.

Movies Come to Vermont

A few Vermonters had seen nickelodeon moving pictures in the early years of the century. In fact, there had even been a movie filmed in Burlington before World War I, but motion pictures were still a rarity in the early spring of 1920 when the school children at recess at White River Junction saw sled loads of strangers arriving at the river's edge in front of the church.

When the bell rang, excited boys and girls could hardly settle down, and a latecomer burst in with the news.

"It's the movie people!" he shouted. "They're going to make a moving picture right here in this town!"

At first nobody believed him, but it turned out to be true.

A famous movie director, D. W. Griffith, and a cast of stars were going to film *Way Down East,* a classic play laid in a New England village.

"The word's going around that they're going to hire local 'extras,'" said someone as the incredible news swept the town.

That turned out to be true, too. Soon the stars, Lillian Gish and Richard Barthelmess, arrived at the local hotel. In a hair-raising scene on the ice, Miss Gish nearly lost her life. Hand-cranked cameras recorded a real rescue that was supposed to have been staged.

This old silent movie, which is still available from film libraries, shows actual Vermont scenes of over half a century ago, giving us a look at old Vermont as well as motion picture history.

Early Radio in Vermont

Something else new came to Vermont after World War I. As early as 1900 newspapers ran stories about Marconi's experiments with wireless, and boys especially were enthralled with the mysterious new discoveries about air waves and sound. Like other boys, teenager Charles Doe tinkered with crystal-set radios and then joined the Navy as a radioman in World War I, where he learned a great deal.

When the war was over, young Charles bought a motorcycle and rode it all the way to Bellows Falls from his home in Boston, putt-putting along on roads that weren't very good and where cars were still rare. Doe found out that there was not a single radio broadcasting station in all of Vermont.

"Why not use the air waves to get news to farmers who

live on remote roads? Immediate weather news would be a godsend to them," the thought flitted through Doe's head.

In 1921, Doe began to install Vermont's first radio broadcasting station in Bellows Falls in the building of the largest farm-machinery company in the area. Of course, there had to be receivers for the broadcasting station, so the company sold radio sets to farmers. Early radios were all individually built, so Charles Doe showed buyers how to put them together.

In September of 1922 Doe made his first broadcast over station WLAK. The Brazil Orchestra from Bellows Falls played music, and Doe gave some advice and relayed news to the farmers.

By today's standards Doe's equipment was simple. He kept the station on the air six hours a day, and a pianist and someone playing gramophone records furnished light entertainment between serious messages.

The first radio sets had many dials to tune to find a station. Radio fans would keep a notebook beside the set to write down the combinations that located a clear station. The first sets had earphones, and people lined up to take turns to listen; even neighbors congregated by the radio, hoping for a chance.

One of the first national radio programs especially for children was the "Uncle Wiggly Bedtime Stories." Youngsters fought for a turn at the earphones to hear the story from the air.

Within a few years there were many more radio stations in Vermont, and the state's first television station, WCAX, was opened in Burlington in 1954.

The first TV set in a town would attract curious and unbelieving people. Pictures sent through the air? What next?

President Calvin Coolidge

PRESIDENT
CALVIN
COOLIDGE

Early in August of 1923 Vice President Calvin Coolidge was visiting his father in Plymouth. That night President Warren Harding died, and when the telegraph message was delivered to the Coolidge home, Calvin Coolidge realized that he was now President of the United States.

"He's got to be sworn in," said one of the neighbors who had come over after seeing the kerosene lamps lit in the Coolidges' parlor. Lamps lit late at night meant some sort of emergency.

"His father is a notary," said one of the newspaper reporters who had heard the telegraphed news in a nearby town and had come along for the story. "His father could administer the oath, for the United States should not be without a President."

So at forty-seven minutes past two o'clock in the morning of August 3, 1923, Colonel John Coolidge administered the oath of office to his son Calvin in the family living room, using the President's mother's Bible. A few hours later President and Mrs. Coolidge got on the special train and went to Washington, where Mr. Coolidge was President until 1929.

While he was President, Calvin Coolidge and his family often came to Vermont to visit, and the President's two sons would help their Grandfather Coolidge with the farm work. Even President Coolidge, a quiet man with a shy sense of humor, would sometimes put on a farmer's "frock"—a garment to protect his clothes—and help with the haying or other chores to show that being a farmer was natural to a Vermonter, even if he was the President of the United States.

The Flood of 1927

In November of 1927 it rained and rained and then it rained some more.

"I don't believe this rain will ever cease," said anxious farmers.

Vermont was used to floods in the spring, but this was something different. Every river, brook, and stream went over its banks, and Vermont had a flood that cut off all communication with the outer world. Before it was over, Vermont's flood disaster destroyed thirty million dollars' worth of property. Small hydro-electric plants, mills, railroads, roads, bridges, and barns with livestock were washed away in the torrents, and forty-five people lost their lives.

Many of the railroads were never restored. Instead, new highways were built for automobiles, which were becoming common now. Instead of rebuilding the small local electric-power plants, larger power plants were built to provide electricity to many towns. Flood-control dams were built to prevent another disaster like the one in 1927.

The Civilian Conservation Corps and the Depression

When the Depression of the 1930's first struck America, Vermont suffered along with the rest of the country. But Vermont still had many small farms where a cow and a garden and an apple tree or so and a woodlot and a hayfield kept people going. Money had always been scarce in Vermont, so people knew how to be frugal.

One of the plans of the American government was to help unemployed young men, especially from the cities, to learn something of woodcraft and country life by enlisting them in the Civilian Conservation Corps. The CCC, as it was known, set up pioneer camps in rural areas, and Vermont was chosen for many of them.

"We need these strong young men to work in our forests," said Perry Merrill, the State Forester. Always conservation-minded, Merrill had been working for years for long-range controls and for improvement in the state's wild lands. Now, with the federal government offering men to do the work, Merrill's dream was about to come true.

Young men between the ages of eighteen and twenty-three, unmarried, without a job, and with good health and character, were allowed to come. Come they did, thousands of them pouring out of big Eastern cities from 1933 to 1942, into the muddy, snowy, bug-ridden, rainy, wild and beautiful backwoods of Vermont. For most of them it was one of the most rewarding experiences of their lives.

Vermont officially had twenty-four CCC camps, although if the special camps and the ones that opened and closed and re-opened were all counted, there were nearly forty camps, many more than any other state had. Young men pruned the forests, built huts, built ski slopes, cleared trails, built roads, repaired bridges, planted seedlings, dammed and dug out streams. In spare moments they snowshoed, learned to ski, built ski jumps, played ball, and studied lessons to finish high school, for many were poor boys who had had to drop out of school. Some even learned to read, for there were a few illiterate men in the group.

Perry Merrill saw to it that the Vermont State Park system was built, conserving choice pieces of wild land for the public. Today people can camp in Vermont's forty-one State Parks, which have neat campsites and clean toilet buildings. Hiking, boating, and swimming are available to anyone who likes the outdoors.

When the CCC camps closed at the beginning of World

War II, Vermont's outdoor life was known to people throughout the country.

The Green Mountain Parkway

While the CCC boys were building trails in the woods and preserving Vermont forests, officials in the United States government thought of a plan to bring quantities of money into Vermont.

"Let's build a national parkway the length of the Green Mountains so people from everywhere can drive along the mountaintops. If lots of cars come, then it will bring prosperity to the state. There are many poor people in Vermont who would be helped by this."

When Vermonters heard about this friendly plan, instead of being overjoyed at the prospect of money pouring in, surprisingly they stopped and thought it over.

"If cars go driving through the Green Mountains, where are we going to hike and hunt?" people asked each other. "It might ruin our Green Mountains to have a road built on them."

People took sides and wrote strong letters to the newspapers.

"It will bring in ten million dollars to Vermont, and think what it would do for the economy," said some.

Finally, in the spring of 1936, the matter was put to a vote by the people at Town Meeting. Town Meeting had not changed much since the days when Vermont was called the New Hampshire Grants. To the surprise of much of the rest of the world, but not to Vermonters, the voters turned down the Green Mountain Parkway.

"Our Green Mountain wilderness is not for sale," decided

the people at the polls. "We'll manage about jobs and money some other way."

From World War II to Act 250

The War

Europe was being torn apart by war in the summer of 1941. Vermont's National Guard had been inducted into federal service in February of that year, and more and more men and women were enlisting, for they knew America would soon be in the fight.

"Vermont has always given her service men a bonus," said someone in the legislature early in 1941. "Let's vote to give each man and woman in service ten dollars a month."

"No," said economy-minded representatives, "we only give that bonus when we are at war."

And so they argued it, and the legislature voted against the extra pay. "We'll give the bonus when war is declared," they decided.

Those were stirring times, when things happened fast. In September of 1941, President Franklin Roosevelt gave "shooting orders" to the United States Navy in case they were attacked on the high seas, even though America was not yet officially in the war.

"We should give our service people a bonus, even if we have to declare war to do it," said some legislators hotly. "Vermont has declared war independently before."

The legislature voted quickly for the bonus, and the world took it to mean that little Vermont had declared war on Germany in September of 1941, ahead of the United States.

The New York Times and the Vermont papers of the day made much of it.

Soon America followed Vermont with a declaration of war after the Japanese attacked Pearl Harbor on December 7, 1941.

Fifty thousand Vermonters served in World War II, of whom twelve thousand were killed. The Reverend George Lansing Fox of Gilman was one of the four chaplains on the *USS Dorchester*. When the ship was torpedoed, Chaplain Fox and three other chaplains lost their lives when they gave their lifejackets to other people, and went down with the ship.

A Poet, and Two Statesmen

ROBERT FROST

ROBERT FROST

The Civil War had been over for almost ten years when a boy was born in San Francisco, California, who was to become a famous citizen of Vermont, the poet Robert Frost.

In 1885, when Robert was eleven years old, his father died, and the boy came across America on the train with his mother and sister to live near relatives in New England. Robert was good at his schoolwork, for his parents had taught him to read and love all sorts of books, including poetry.

Because the family had little money, the boy worked at a variety of jobs, from shoemaker's helper to farm chores. His natural curiosity made him look deeply into the wonders of what seemed to others merely the everyday world around him. When he was in high school he began to write down some of his thoughts in poetry which was published in the school paper.

When Robert Frost married his high school sweetheart several years later, a few magazines were already publishing his poems. Before many more years passed, he went on to become one of America's, and finally one of the world's, best-known modern poets. When he moved to Vermont in 1919 he wrote poems about the land and the deep meaning he saw in the daily life of his neighbors and himself, and his poems made children as well as scholars aware of a special way of looking at things.

Once he said, "Spring flowers are so slow to come in New England. One year I made some out of paper and put them on the roads on April Fool's Day. . . ."

When Robert Frost died in 1963 his spirit was left forever as a part of the Green Mountain State.

WARREN AUSTIN

WARREN AUSTIN

When Warren Austin entered the University of Vermont as a young man, he was deeply conscious of the Canadian border that lay close by. He had been aware of Vermont's international situation since he was a small boy in Highgate, where he was born in 1877, and he was determined to spend some of his vacations in Quebec learning about our "foreign" neighbor, Canada.

Austin graduated and became a lawyer like his father, but he continued to think about matters beyond the borders of Vermont. A chance came for him to see a great deal of the world when, in 1915, he was asked to go to China to give business and legal advice about railroads.

In 1931 Warren Austin was elected to the United States Senate, where he was able to use his influence in foreign policy. He was a valuable statesman in the stirring days of the New Deal of President Franklin D. Roosevelt; sometimes he disagreed with the President, but he always had Mr. Roosevelt's respect. As World War II began in Europe in 1939, he made a strong stand that America must not be an "isolationist" country, but instead must take a leading role in world affairs.

When the war was over and the United Nations was being established to try to keep peace in the world, Senator Austin had a significant part in helping draft the charter of the organization of countries. President Harry Truman appointed him as America's first Ambassador to the United Nations. Warren Austin died in 1962, and the world knew that the boy from Highgate had been one of the most important men of the 20th Century.

GEORGE D. AIKEN

GEORGE AIKEN

George Aiken was born in 1892, and as a boy he found deep joy in the wildflowers that abounded on his father's farm in Putney. Looking at them, he determined to save as many of them as he could from being destroyed. Shortly after young George graduated from Brattleboro High School he borrowed one hundred dollars to plant a patch of raspberries which grew to five hundred acres. Soon he added a nursery, and the boy-naturalist built a career as a farmer and expert on wildflowers and small fruits and berries.

In 1936 George Aiken was elected Governor of Vermont, but he did not lose his interest in the world of nature. When he was elected to the United States Senate in 1940 he served for thirty-five years, but he never lost his neighborly spirit.

Senator Aiken, always outspoken and independent, had the support of Vermont behind him as he championed the rights of people and the land. In the Senate he worked hard for agriculture programs that would help his country's farmers and world food supplies, too, and he supported foreign aid to underdeveloped countries. Like Senator Austin, he was concerned with the foreign policy of the United States, believing that America must not isolate herself. He disliked giant businesses, especially the complicated utility companies, and he worked always for the sensible rights of individuals.

During the years he lived in Washington, Senator Aiken came to Vermont each month to talk and listen to his neighbors, Democrats and Republicans alike. In Washington he was often seen feeding the pigeons in the park, for he lived as simply in the nation's capital as he did on his farm before his fellow citizens sent him there to represent them.

George Aiken has been a friend and advisor to six Presidents in his political career, and, said a national newspaper, "No man in America has made a larger contribution to the betterment of American rural life than George Aiken."

George Aiken's sense of humor shines through to every country child in Vermont on the first page of his book *Pioneering with Wild Flowers*, which reads:

> Dedicated to Peter Rabbit in the hope that flattery will accomplish what traps and guns have failed to do and that the little rascal will let our plants alone from this time on.

Vermont, the Beckoning Country

After World War II was over, many people looked to Vermont for a new kind of life, a life of peace and clean air. Land was cheap and there were still old farms to be had where an industrious family could make a living.

Skiing and other winter sports were catching on. So many things beckoned people to the Green Mountains that land prices began to soar, farms were cut up into lots for vacation homes, and people demanded more roads and electricity and public services. Two interstate highways were begun, and highways were often jammed with carloads of visitors. To meet the need for a lot more electricity, an atomic power plant was built on the Connecticut River at Vernon, causing arguments and indignation meetings because some people wanted it and some didn't.

So many people came to Vermont to live that the state's leaders were troubled. The population jumped from 378,000 in 1950 to 444,000 in 1970. Old people, young people, poor people, rich people, all flocked to Vermont. Young people who were often called "hippies" arrived in droves to become Vermonters and live close to the earth like the pioneers of two hundred years before.

Vermont had weathered many problems since 1777. Her people had fought and planned and struggled and sacrificed to keep Vermont a good place to live. Would the life all go down the drain now, because the land was developed to death?

Governor Deane C. Davis and the Vermont legislature took a look at the serious problems of too much development and vanishing farms. "Why don't we set up some strong laws to protect the environment and control the development of the state?" they asked each other. "Doesn't our Constitution say that the private use of property is not as important as the public good? Didn't our people turn down the prosperity of the Green Mountain Parkway rather than spoil our Green Mountains?"

"No state has ever done it before," argued some.

"It's too radical," said others.

All through the year of 1969, dedicated men and women worked to come up with a fair law to present to the legislature for a vote. How would the lawmakers decide?

The End, and a Beginning

The page boy had finished his errands and was hurrying away for his lunch when the class filed out of the State House gallery.

"Well, as you see, they passed the environmental laws," he said to the teacher who stopped him to ask the way to the cafeteria.

Reporters buttonholed some of the lawmakers who were leaving their desks as the morning session ended.

"What's this going to mean to Vermont?" asked one reporter, his pencil poised to write down the answer.

"It's the end of wild development, I believe," said one legislator.

"I think it's a beginning, too," said another. "Vermont is a state with a true storybook past, and now perhaps she can look forward to a storybook future."

Acknowledgments

The Molly Robinson diary is used by permission of the Rowland E. Robinson Memorial Association.

The Life of Elias Smith is used by permission of the Vermont Historical Society.

Material on Ezra Brainerd from family records is courtesy of Mrs. Catherine Eddy of Middlebury.

Henry Little's letter appeared in the St. *Johnsbury Caledonian* of March 9, 1883.

Rowland Robinson's "Recollections of a Quaker Boy" appeared in the *Atlantic Monthly* of July 1901.

Robert Louis Stevenson's letter to Annie Ide is used by permission of the Fairbanks Museum of Natural Science at St. Johnsbury.

My special thanks go to Dr. H. N. Muller III of the University of Vermont History Department who encouraged, instructed, and advised me along the way and laboriously combed the finished manuscript for possible errors.

I also want to thank the staff of the Vermont Historical Society, especially Mrs. Laura Abbott, who aided and abetted as I dug through masses of material in the VHS Library.

Col. John A. Williams, Editor of State Papers, in the office of Secretary of State, gave me hours of help and made the Vermont Archives available to me repeatedly, for which I am very grateful.

The staff of the Wilbur Collection at the Billings Library at the University of Vermont provided me with books, manuscripts, and attention above the call of duty. I also wish to thank Dr. William Haviland and Dr. Philip Wagner of the UVM faculty for advice in matters pertaining to Indians and the geological structure of Vermont.

My thanks also to Edward and Janet Williams for use of manuscript material and hospitality at "Rokeby," the home of Rowland E. Robinson, where they served as curators.

The St. Michael's College Library, with the special help of librarian Mary Rivard, made many otherwise unavailable books accessible to me from its shelves and from loan sources, for which I am grateful.

Thanks to staff members at all Vermont libraries, especially the State Library at Montpelier, the Brooks Memorial Library at Brattleboro, the Sheldon Museum Library and the Middlebury College Library at Middlebury, the Fairbanks Museum of Natural Science at St. Johnsbury, the Proctor Free Library at Proctor, and to Gertrude Mallary of Fairlee who made her splendid personal collection of Vermontiana available to me throughout my research.

Thanks to the many people who took time to tell me about their own experiences in Vermont, and to staff members at the Vermont Education Department who advised me and provided information.

Finally, I am beholden to the Vermont Bicentennial Commission for help in the form of a research grant to help me write this book, and to the members of their Publications Committee for their careful reading, advice, and recommendation.

Appendix I

An Explanation of Act 250

Historically, Vermont took a stand on the public's interest in private property when the first Constitution stated: "Private property ought to be subservient to public uses when necessity requires it."

By 1970, uncontrolled development had produced such an effect on Vermont's fragile environment that the 1970 legislative session passed laws to control the abuse of Vermont's natural heritage in a unique piece of legislation known as "Act 250." Under this State Land Use and Development statute, permits are required for any substantial development, public or private. To obtain a permit, a developer or land subdivider must show that the land is suitable for the proposed project and that it will have no adverse effect on the surroundings. This law differs from the traditional zoning concept, which allocates land to specific uses.

District Environmental Commissions appointed by the Governor consider applications and may issue permits to comply with the following criteria:

Will air and water be polluted?

Is there sufficient water for the proposed project?

Will there be a burden on existing water supplies?

Can roads and other transportation handle the increased traffic?

Can schools accommodate an increased population?

Can the community provide municipal services?

Will scenic beauty, historic sites, wildlife, and irreplaceable natural areas be abused?

The Act provided that development must comply with local and regional plans, and called for a Land Capability Plan which was passed in 1973. A Land Use Plan is under consideration at this writing (1976).

A nine-member State Environmental Board, also appointed by the Governor, acts as a court of appeals above the local commissions. Act 250 does not regulate subdivisions of less than ten lots, or residential construction of less than ten units.

Appendix II

A Chronology

Date	Vermont	North America

8000 B.C. About 10,000 years ago Paleo Indians are believed to have been living in Vermont and other parts of North America, probably having come from Asia across the Bering Straits. About 6,000 to 3,000 years ago Archaic or Pre-Woodland Indians were here, followed by Woodland Indians about 3,000 to 2,000 years ago to modern times.

A.D. 1000   *Vikings from Iceland established a colony in North America.*

1300–1750 Abnaki and Iroquois Indians roamed Vermont.   *Columbus discovered America (1492).*
Jacques Cartier, French explorer, discovered the St. Lawrence River (1534).

1564 Johne Graye may have visited the banks of the Missisquoi River.

1609 Samuel de Champlain entered Vermont with Abnaki Indians and fought the Iroquois.   *Henry Hudson, seeking a North-west Passage for the Dutch, entered the Hudson River.*
The Pilgrims landed at Plymouth Bay, Massachusetts (1620).

1646 Father Isaac Jogues, Jesuit missionary, was slain by Mohawk Indians.   *French traders and colonists came to Canada hoping to establish a French empire in North America (1632–1763).*

Date   *Vermont*   *North America*

1666   The French built a fort and shrine to Ste. Anne at Isle la Motte.

1676   French seigneuries were first granted along Lake Champlain.

King Philip's War was fought between Indians and settlers on the New England frontier (1675–78).

1689   Indians, disturbed by encroaching Europeans, fought each other and raided white settlements in Massachusetts near Vermont's present border.

King William's War (1689–97), first phase of the French and Indian wars, pitted the French and Abnaki against the English and Iroquois.

1704   Deerfield, Massachusetts, was raided by Abnaki, and 119 prisoners were marched to Canada through Vermont. Reverend John Williams preached a sermon in Rockingham where the prisoners camped.

Queen Anne's War (1702–13) was the second phase of the French and Indian wars.

1724   Fort Dummer, the first permanent English settlement in Vermont, was built at Brattleboro.
From 1700 to 1750 the Abnaki Chief Greylock fought the English, hoping to drive them from Vermont.

1726   Timothy Dwight, Vermont's first known native white child, was born at Fort Dummer.

King George's War (1744–48) was fought in the colonies.

1749   Governor Benning Wentworth of New Hampshire made the first land grant, chartering the town of Bennington.

1754   "Captive" Johnson was born in Windsor County after her mother's capture from Fort Number 4.

1,196 English colonists were captured and taken to Canada by the Indians between 1689 and 1762.

Date	Vermont	North America
1759	Hope of peace made Vermont safer for settlement. Wentworth had granted 15 towns, which had not yet been settled.	*The last phase of the French and Indian wars was fought (1755–62).* *Robert Rogers and his Rangers destroyed the St. Francis Indian stronghold in Canada (1759). Montcalm and Wolfe both died at Quebec. The victory for England turned the tide of the colonial wars.*
1760	The Crown Point Military Road was built. Vermont's non-Indian population was 300.	*George III was crowned King of England (1760–1820).*
1761	Settlers began moving into Bennington, Guilford, Halifax, Newbury, Pawlet, and Townshend.	
1763	France relinquished claims to Vermont in the Treaty of Paris, which ended the wars between France and England.	*France ceded all her land in North America east of the Mississippi to Great Britain. Spain gave Florida to Great Britain.*
1764	King George set the Connecticut River as boundary between New Hampshire and New York, favoring New York and voiding the Hampshire Grants.	
1765	Vermont's non-Indian population was 1,000.	*The Stamp Act was protested in the English colonies.*
1766	Bennington sent representative Samuel Robinson to London to protest New York's boundary claims.	
1769	Bennington settlers drove out surveyors from New York.	
1770	Ethan Allen arrived in the Grants and was chosen to represent the people in their fight against New York claims.	*The Boston Massacre killed five people in Boston.* *The population of the English colonies was 2,205,000.*

Date	Vermont	North America
1771	Vermont's non-Indian population was 4,669.	
1774	The Westminster meeting in October supported the Continental Congress.	*The Boston Tea Party protested the three-penny tax on tea (December of 1773).* *The Continental Congress met in Philadelphia in September of 1774.*
1775	The Westminster "Massacre" happened in March. Ethan Allen took Fort Ticonderoga in May. Seth Warner captured Crown Point. Benedict Arnold seized a British sloop. The June convention at Dorset elected Seth Warner head of the Green Mountain Boys. Ethan Allen, as a volunteer scout, tried to take Montreal, failed, and was captured (to be imprisoned in England until 1778).	*The Battle of Lexington and Concord began the Revolution in April.* *George Washington took command of Continental troops in July.* *The Americans were defeated at Quebec in December. Montgomery was killed, Benedict Arnold was wounded.*
1776	Four important conventions were held: at Dorset in January, July, and September, and at Westminster in October. Fort Independence was built on Lake Champlain opposite Fort Ticonderoga. The Battle of Valcour in October delayed the English advance down Lake Champlain.	*The Declaration of Independence was signed in Philadelphia on July 4.*
1777	Vermont declared independence on January 17 at Westminster. "New Connecticut" was chosen as the new republic's first name. Vermont got her present name at Windsor on June 4. At a meeting in Windsor on July 2, the Vermont Constitution was adopted and a Council of Safety	*The Stars and Strips was adopted by Congress on June 14. The new flag had 13 stars and 13 stripes. Burgoyne began moving south from Canada in June.*

Date *Vermont*

North America

was set up to govern, headed by Thomas Chittenden. Ira Allen was Secretary of State. The Council moved to Bennington. Fort Ticonderoga and Fort Independence were evacuated on July 6.
Battle of Hubbardton, July 7, was a victory for the British.
Battle of Bennington, August 16, defeated the British, who fell back farther into New York.

In July, New Hampshire sent General Stark and troops to help beleaguered Vermont. Burgoyne surrendered at Saratoga in October.

1778 The first general elections were held. The Assembly met at Windsor on March 12 with delegates elected by the towns. Thomas Chittenden was elected Governor. Ethan Allen returned from captivity in England.

1778–82 New Hampshire, New York, and Vermont made frequent boundary changes. The Vermont Assembly quarreled over the questions of boundaries and of admission to the United States. The Haldimand Affair involved Vermont in intrigue with Great Britain (1780–83).

British General Cornwallis surrendered to Washington at Yorktown on October 19, 1781.

1783 Vermont's first newspaper, the *Vermont Gazette,* was published in Bennington.

The Treaty of Paris officially ended the American Revolution.

1784 Postal service was established in five towns.
Ethan Allen published his book on deism, *Reason, the Only Oracle of Man.*

1785 Vermont made copper coins and issued paper money.

Date	Vermont	North America
1786	Vermonters attempted to stop courts from prosecuting debt cases.	*Shay's Rebellion took place in western Massachusetts (1786–87). The United States Constitution was ratified (1787).*
1789	Vermont and New York appointed a special commission to settle the border controversy.	
1790	The Vermont–New York boundary was settled. Vermont's population was 85,425; Guilford the largest town (2,432).	
1791	In January, Vermont delegates met in a special assembly at Bennington to vote for statehood. March 4, Vermont was admitted to the Union as the 14th State. Justin Morgan purchased the horse that became the foundation sire of the Morgan breed. The University of Vermont was chartered at the instigation of Ira Allen. The University opened in 1800.	*The Bill of Rights was added to the United States Constitution.*
1792	A canal was built at Bellows Falls to bypass the falls on the Connecticut River.	*Kentucky entered the Union as the 15th State.*
1793	The first copper mine in the United States was opened at Strafford.	
1797	Thomas Chittenden died.	
1800	Vermont's population was 154,396, an 80% increase over 1790.	*George Washington died (1799). Population of the United States was 5,308,483.*
1805	Montpelier became the permanent capital of Vermont.	*The United States placed an embargo on British goods (1807).*

Date	Vermont	North America
1811	Vermonters engaged in smuggling with Canada to avoid the embargo. William Jarvis introduced merino sheep from Spain.	*United States declared war on Britain (1812).*
1814	Thomas Macdonough defeated the British on Lake Champlain.	*The War of 1812 ended (1815).*
1815–60	A period of great social ferment in Vermont and the United States. Temperance, anti-slavery, and religious revival movements flourished. Mechanical inventions changed people's lives.	
1816	The Year Without a Summer.	
1820	Vermont's population was 235,966. Windsor was the largest town.	*Northern states protested the admission of Missouri to the Union.*
1825	Lafayette visited Vermont.	*The Erie Canal was completed.*
1830	Chester A. Arthur was born at Fairfield.	*Joseph Smith founded the Church of Jesus Christ of Latter-day Saints at Fayette, New York.*
1833	The second State House was built at Montpelier.	*The United States entered a period of wild speculation in public land, roads, canals, and banks (1833–37).*
1836	Vermont changed to a bicameral legislature (the Governor's Council became the Senate).	*Financial panic began (1837). In the first year, 618 banks failed, starting a seven-year depression.*
1838	Imprisonment for debt became illegal in Vermont.	
1840	Vermont's population was 291,948. Burlington was the largest town. John Humphrey Noyes established his utopian community at Putney (later moved to New York). Daniel Webster spoke on Stratton Mountain.	*Charles Dickens visited America (1842).* *United States declared war with Mexico (1846).* *Gold was discovered in California (1848).*

Date	Vermont	North America
1848–49	Vermont's first railroads were built, Rutland to Burlington, and White River Junction to Bethel.	*Treaty with Mexico established the Rio Grande River as boundary and gained much of the Southwest for the United States.*
1858	In defiance of the Federal Fugitive Slave Law, Vermont freed all blacks who had been brought into the state.	
1860	Vermont's population was 315,098, with Burlington still the largest town.	*Abraham Lincoln was elected President.* *South Carolina seceded from the Union, and soon was followed by other Southern states.*
1861	Vermont was the first state to offer troops in the Civil War. Half the eligible men in the state served.	*The Civil War began.*
1864	Confederates raided St. Albans.	*The Civil War ended (1865). Abraham Lincoln was assassinated (April 14, 1865).*
1866–70	Irish Fenians, based in Vermont, invaded Canada.	*The first transcontinental railroad was completed, with ceremonies at Promontory Point, Utah (1869).*
1872	Calvin Coolidge was born at Plymouth.	
1880	Vermont's population was 332,286.	
1894	The Red Clover was named the State Flower.	*Geronimo, an Apache chief, was captured, ending the last major Indian war (1886).*
1900	Vermont's population was 343,641.	*Population of United States was 75,994,575.*
1902	The operation of motor vehicles was restricted by law.	*Approximately 8,000 automobiles were in operation in the United States (1900).*

Date   *Vermont*   *North America*

1910	Vermont's first airplane flight took place. The Long Trail was begun.	*The Panama Canal was formally opened to traffic (1914).*
1916	16,000 Vermont men enlisted to fight in World War I.	*The United States entered World War I.*
1920	Vermont's population was 352,-428.	*The Eighteenth Amendment (Prohibition) was ratified (1919).* *The Nineteenth Amendment (Women's Suffrage) was ratified (1920).* *Calvin Coolidge became the thirtieth President.*
1927	A destructive flood hit Vermont.	
1934	The first ski tow in the United States was built at Woodstock, Vermont.	*America and Europe suffered in the Great Depression (1929–38). Prohibition ended (1934).*
1940	Vermont's population was 359,-231.	
1941	Vermont voted a bonus for service men in September.	*The United States entered World War II in December.*
1954	Consuelo N. Bailey became the nation's first elected woman Lieutenant Governor. The state's first television broadcasting station was built on Mount Mansfield.	*In Brown v. Board of Education, the Supreme Court ruled that racial segregation in public schools is unconstitutional.* *The first American satellite, Explorer I, was launched into orbit (1958).*
1960	Vermont's population was 389,-881.	
1970	Vermont's population was 444,-732, an increase of 14.1% over 1960. The Vermont legislature passed Act 250, a landmark in environmental legislation.	*United States population was 203,810,000.*

Appendix III

Some Facts About Vermont

Statehood: Vermont became the Fourteenth State on March 4, 1791, after being an independent republic since January 17, 1777.

Capital: Montpelier, chosen as Vermont's permanent seat of government in 1805.

Coat-of-arms: A pine tree in a pastoral setting, mountains in the background, with the motto "Vermont: Freedom and Unity."

Nickname: "Green Mountain State," from the French words *verd mont,* meaning "green mountain."

Special days: Town Meeting day, which is the first Tuesday in March; Bennington Battle Day, August 16.

State Symbols

Animal: Morgan horse.
Bird: Hermit thrush.
Flag: Blue, with the Vermont coat-of-arms in the center.
Flower: Red clover.
Song: "Hail Vermont."
Tree: Sugar maple.
More information about these symbols can be found in the *Vermont Legislative Directory and State Manual* issued by Vermont's Secretary of State.

Some Geography

Area: 9,609 square miles.
Population: 444,732 (1970 census).
Longitude: 71° 33' to 73° 25' West.

Latitude: 42° 44′ to 45° 43′ North.
Physical size: Length north to south, 158 miles; northern boundary, 90 miles; southern boundary, 40 miles.
Political units: Vermont has 14 counties; 9 cities; 237 organized towns; 5 unorganized towns; 4 gores.
Cities: In the 1970 census, its largest cities are, in descending order, Burlington, Rutland, Barre, South Burlington, and Montpelier.
Towns: Vermont's largest towns are Bennington, Brattleboro, Essex, Springfield, and Colchester.

Some Natural Features

Mountains: Vermont's ten highest mountains are Mansfield Chin (4,393 alt.), Killington, Camels Hump, Mount Ellen, Abraham, Cutts Peak, Mansfield Nose, Lincoln, Pico, and Little Killington.
Rivers: The longest river within the state's borders is Otter Creek, followed in size by Winooski, Lamoille, White, and Missisquoi rivers. The mighty Connecticut River only forms Vermont's eastern boundary: New Hampshire actually has jurisdiction over its waters.
Lakes: The largest lakes in order of length are Champlain, Memphremagog (these two only partly in Vermont), Bomoseen, Willoughby, Carmi, St. Catherine, and Seymour.
Flowers: Gentian, aster, bloodroot, cattail, dutchmen's breeches, lady's-slipper, lupine, trillium, jack-in-the-pulpit, pitcher plant, bog orchid, Solomon's-seal.
Trees: Most common are maple, ash, beech, birch, oak, elm, tamarack, pine, spruce, fir, hemlock, cedar.
Animals: Among others, raccoon, deer, catamount (now extinct), squirrel, woodchuck, porcupine, coyote, bear, beaver, otter, moose, skunk.
Birds: Owl, oriole, cardinal, chickadee, robin, finch, grosbeak, woodpecker, nuthatch, hummingbird, bluebird, martin, quail, jay, goose, loon, and many more.
Fish: Perch, trout, bass, bream, eel, salmon, catfish, sheepshead, carp, and more.
Reptiles: Tortoise, snake, turtle.

Vermont Governors, 1778–1976

Thomas Chittenden	1778–1789	Paul Brigham	1797
Moses Robinson	1789–1790	Isaac Tichenor	1797–1807
Thomas Chittenden	1790–1797	Israel Smith	1807–1808

Isaac Tichenor	1808–1809	Ebenezer J. Ormsbee	1886–1888
Jonas Galusha	1809–1813	William P. Dillingham	1888–1890
Martin Chittenden	1813–1815	Carroll S. Page	1890–1892
Jonas Galusha	1815–1820	Levi K. Fuller	1892–1894
Richard Skinner	1820–1823	Urban A. Woodbury	1894–1896
Cornelius P. Van Ness	1823–1826	Josiah Grout	1896–1898
Ezra Butler	1826–1828	Edward C. Smith	1898–1900
Samuel C. Crafts	1828–1831	William W. Stickney	1900–1902
William A. Palmer	1831–1835	John G. McCullough	1902–1904
Silas H. Jennison	1835–1841	Charles J. Bell	1904–1906
Charles Paine	1841–1843	Fletcher D. Proctor	1906–1908
John Mattocks	1843–1844	George H. Prouty	1908–1910
William Slade	1844–1846	John A. Mead	1910–1912
Horace Eaton	1846–1848	Allen M. Fletcher	1912–1915
Carlos Coolidge	1848–1850	Charles W. Gates	1915–1917
Charles K. Williams	1850–1852	Horace F. Graham	1917–1919
Erastus Fairbanks	1852–1853	Percival W. Clement	1919–1921
John S. Robinson	1853–1854	James Hartness	1921–1923
Stephen Royce	1854–1856	Redfield Proctor	1923–1925
Ryland Fletcher	1856–1858	Franklin S. Billings	1925–1927
Hiland Hall	1858–1860	John E. Weeks	1927–1931
Erastus Fairbanks	1860–1861	Stanley C. Wilson	1931–1935
Frederick Holbrook	1861–1863	Charles M. Smith	1935–1937
J. Gregory Smith	1863–1865	George D. Aiken	1937–1941
Paul Dillingham	1865–1867	William H. Wills	1941–1945
John B. Page	1867–1869	Mortimer R. Proctor	1945–1947
Peter T. Washburn	1869–1870	Ernest W. Gibson	1947–1950
George W. Hendee	1870	Harold J. Arthur	1950–1951
John W. Stewart	1870–1872	Lee E. Emerson	1951–1955
Julius Converse	1872–1874	Joseph B. Johnson	1955–1959
Asahel Peck	1874–1876	Robert T. Stafford	1959–1961
Horace Fairbanks	1876–1878	F. Ray Keyser, Jr.	1961–1963
Redfield Proctor	1878–1880	Philip H. Hoff	1963–1969
Roswell Farnham	1880–1882	Deane C. Davis	1969–1973
John L. Barstow	1882–1884	Thomas P. Salmon	1973–
Samuel E. Pingree	1884–1886		

Appendix IV

Some Books About Vermont

FICTION:

Cheney, Cora. *The Doll of Lilac Valley*. New York: Alfred Knopf, 1959.

Coblentz, Catherine Cate. *The Blue Cat of Castle Town*. Taftsville, Vt.: The Countryman Press, 1974.

Fisher, Dorothy Canfield. *Understood Betsy*. New York: Holt, Rinehart, and Winston, 1972.

Hill, Ralph Nading. *The Voyages of Brian Seaworthy*. Montpelier, Vt.: Vermont Life Magazine and the Vermont Historical Society, 1971.

Kelley, Shirley. *Little Settlers of Vermont*. Orford, N.H.: Equity, 1963.

Otto, Margaret. *Mr. Kipling's Elephant*. New York: Alfred Knopf, 1961.

Thompson, Mary W. *Two in the Wilderness*. New York: David McKay, 1967.

Viereck, Philip. *Independence Must Be Won*. New York: John Day, 1964.

Wriston, Hildreth. *Susan's Secret*. New York: Farrar-Straus, 1957.

HISTORY AND POLITICS:

Hill, Ralph Nading. *Contrary Country*. Brattleboro, Vt.: The Stephen Greene Press, 1961.

Hoyt, Edwin P. *The Damndest Yankees: Ethan Allen and His Clan*. Brattleboro, Vt.: The Stephen Greene Press, 1976.

Smith, Bradford. *Rogers' Rangers and the French and Indian Wars*. New York: Random House Landmark Series, 1956.

Vermont Legislative Directory and State Manual. Montpelier, Vt.: The Office of the Secretary of State, 1975 (prepared biennially).

NATURE AND GEOGRAPHY:

Aiken, George D. *Pioneering with Wildflowers*. Englewood Cliffs, N.J.: Prentice-Hall, 1963.

Daniels, Thomas E. *Vermont Indians*. Poultney, Vt.: Journal Press, 1963.

Huden, John. *Archeology in Vermont*. Rutland, Vt.: Charles E. Tuttle, 1971.

Jacobs, E. C. *The Physical Features of Vermont*. Montpelier, Vt.: Vermont State Development Department, 1969.

Mellin, Jeanne. *The Morgan Horse*. Brattleboro, Vt.: The Stephen Greene Press, 1961.

Rood, Ronald, et al. *The Vermont Life Book of Nature*. Brattleboro, Vt.: The Stephen Greene Press, 1967.

Thompson, Zadock. *Natural History of Vermont*. Rutland, Vt.: Charles E. Tuttle, 1971.

The Vermont Yearbook, 1976. Chester, Vt.: The National Survey, 1976.

CRAFTS BOOKS FROM THE PAST:

Beard, D. C. *The American Boys Handy Book*. Rutland, Vt.: Charles E. Tuttle, 1966.

Beard, Lina, and Adelia B. Beard. *The American Girls Handy Book*. Rutland, Vt.: Charles E. Tuttle, 1969.

POETRY:

Frost, Robert. *Robert Frost: His Poetry and Prose*. Lathem, Edward C. and Thompson, Lawrence, eds. New York: Holt, Rinehart, and Winston, 1973.

About the Author

Cora Cheney, who lives at South Windham, Vermont, has written many books for children as well as numerous magazine and newspaper stories for adults. Always interested in history, in the 1970's she turned her attention to an intensive research of Vermont history, winning a Bicentennial grant that helped her uncover new material of special interest to young readers.

Here for the first time is a history of Vermont from prehistoric times to the passage in 1970 of "Act 250," which has received nationwide attention as a landmark in environmental quality control. The book is packed with true stories of Vermonters of all ages, but with a point of view especially intended for young people.

In private life Cora Cheney is Mrs. Benjamin W. Partridge, Jr., and is the mother of four children. Mrs. Partridge is an active member of her local school and library committees and is a trustee of the Vermont Historical Society.

Index

Abercromby, James 25
Abnaki Indians 8–12, 18–19
Act 250 1–2, 205–206, 209–10
   See also Land use
Adams, Dr. Samuel 40
Adams, President John 95–96
Adams, President John Quincy
   125
Addison County (Vt.) 171
Agriculture 127, 176, 203–204
Aiken, George D. 203–204; *ill. 203*
Algonquin Indians 8–9
   See also Abnaki
Allen, Ethan 81–82, 95, 97, 104,
   112; *ill. 37*
   in Canada 57–60
   Haldimand Plot 83–85
   land dispute with New York 33–
   45, 48, 87–88
   at Ticonderoga 50–56
Allen, Fanny 97
Allen, Heman 63–64, 67
Allen, Ira 37, 40, 73, 74–76, 84,
   117, 149; *ill. 74*
Allen, Levi 42
American Revolution 49–88 *pas-
   sim*
   See also Allen, Ethan; Arnold,
   Benedict; Green Mountain
   Boys; Ticonderoga

Amherst, Jeffery 25–26
AMTRAK 183
Andover (Vt.) 156
Archaic Indians 7–8
Arlington (Vt.) 31
Arnold, Benedict 84
   Battle of Valcour 64–66
   in Canada 60–61
   at Ticonderoga 52–56
Arthur, Chester 168; *ill. 168*
Assembly (Vt.) 78–80, 121–22,
   150, 200–201
   See also Government (Vt.)
Austin, Warren 202–203; *ill. 202*
Automobiles 179–81, 190
Aviation 189–90

Bailey, Consuelo Northrup 193
Baker, Remember 37, 39–40
Barnet 128
Barre (Vt.) 157, 180, 187–88
Barton, General William 117
Battell, Joseph 127
Battle(s)
   Bennington 76–78
   Gettysburg 138
   Hubbardton 71
   Saratoga 78
   Valcour 64–66
Bayley, Jacob 62, 67

Beach, Samuel 51–52
Beard, Edna 192
Bedell, Henry 144–47
Beeman, Nathan 53–54
Bellows Falls 120, 159, 194–95
Bennington 82, 134
  Battle of 76–78
  first settlers in 29–31
Bentley, Wilson "Snowflake" 183–85
Bill of Rights (Vt.) 72
Blacks (in Vt.) 149–51
  See also Slavery; Underground Railroad
Blackboard(s), in schools 119
Boundary disputes (Vt.–N.Y.–N.H.) 29, 31–41, 45–49, 63, 66–67, 79–81, 86–88
Bowker, Joseph 73
Boyce, Phoebe 102
Brainerd, Ezra 135
Brattleboro (Vt.) 86, 134, 161, 162–63, 174, 179, 182, 186
Breakenridge, James 33, 38–39
Bridgman's Fort 23
Brookfield (Vt.) 119
Brown, John 59–60
Brownington Academy 150
Burgoyne, General John 69–71, 76–78
Burlington (Vt.) 159, 182, 195
Burnham, Carrie (Mrs. Kilgore) 170
Burnham, John 82

Caledonia County (Vt.) 149
Camp Vail 191
Canada
  during Civil War 134–35, 141–42, 144
expedition against (1775) 57–61
  Fenian raid against 155
  Rebellion against England 110
  in 20th Century 182, 191, 202
Canals 128
Captivity of Mrs. Johnson, The 22–23
Carillon, Fort 25
Carleton, Sir Guy 59
Carpenter, Isaiah 35
Carpenter, Zephaniah 151
Catamount Tavern 33–34, 36–40 passim; ill. 34
Celts (in Vt.) 13–14
Champlain, Lake 4–5, 10, 11, 128–29
  in American Revolution 64–66, 69–70, 79, 84
  in War of 1812 105–106
Champlain, Samuel de 11–12, 17; ill. 11
Chandler, Judge Thomas 46–48
Children, role of 41–43, 89–93, 116–19, 177–79
Chimney Point (Vt.) 16–17
Chittenden, Lucius E. 147
Chittenden, Thomas 67–69, 74–75, 78, 83–85, 89, 93, 95; ill. 78
Church of Jesus Christ of Latter-day Saints 113–14
Churches, see Religion
Circus (in Vt.) 164
Civil War 133–47
Civilian Conservation Corps (CCC) 197–98
Clinton, George 86–88
Cochran, Robert 37, 40
Colburn, Amanda 144
Colburn, Zerah 100–101

Colden, Cadwallader 31–35; *ill.*
  31
Connecticut Courant 38
Connecticut River 4–5, 128–29
Conservationists (Vt.) 151, 169–
  70
Constitution (Vt.) 1, 69, 71–73,
  111, 133, 172, 205
Continental Congress 45–46, 57,
  67
Coolidge, Calvin 165–66, 196
Cooper, Clara 188–89
Coos Indians 8
Council of Safety (Vt.) 73
Courts, *see* Judiciary
Craftsbury (Vt.) 170
Crocker, Sewall 181
Crown Point 55
Crown Point Military Road 25
"Cumberland War" 86–88

Dairying 176
Davenport, Henry 139
Davenport, Thomas 98–99
Davis, Deane 188, 205
Debtors, problems of 89, 116–17
Declaration of Independence
  (U.S.) 61–62
Deerfield (Mass.), Indian raid on
  19–20
Defiance, Mount 70
Delaplace, Captain William 54–
  55
Depression (1930's) 197–98
Dewey, Admiral George 175–76,
  192–93
Disease, *see* Medicine
Doe, Charles 194–95
Dorrilites 112
Dummer, Fort 20–21

Dummer, William 20
Dwight, Timothy 20–21

Education 41, 117–19, 142, 151,
  161, 167–68
Ellis, Joel 164–65
Emigration (from Vt.) 114, 131–
  32, 147
England
  Haldimand Plot 83–85
  settlers from, in Vt. 17–26, 149
  war with American colonies 49–
    56, 59–62, 64–66, 69–73, 76–
    78, 88–89
Environment, concern for 1–2, 72,
  151, 169–70, 199–200, 205–
  206, 209–10
Erie Canal 128
Estey, Jacob (organ-maker) 162–
  63
Experiment in International Liv-
  ing 161
Explorers (of Vt.) 11–15
Extension Service 188, 191

Fairbanks, Erastus 137
Fairbanks Museum 173
Fairbanks, Thaddeus 99–100
Fairfield (Vt.) 168
Fanny Allen Hospital 97
Fay, John 77
Fay, Dr. Jonas 36, 39, 67
Fay, Stephen 36
Fenian Society 155
Ferrisburg (Vt.) 177
Finns (in Vt.) 156
Fisher, Dorothy Canfield 192
Flood, of 1927 182, 197
Fort(s)
  Bridgman's 23

Fort(s) (*Cont.*)
  Carillon 25
  Dummer 20–21
  Independence 61–62, 70
  Number Four 22
  St. Frederic 16–17
  St. Johns 55–56
  Ste. Anne 16
  Ticonderoga 25, 50–55, 70
4-H Club(s) 188, 191
Fox, Rev. George Lansing 201
Franchise, *see* Voting
France
  explorers from, in Vt. 11–17
  settlers from, in Vt. 14–17, 149,
    152–53
Franco–Americans, *see* French–
  Canadians
French
  –Canadians, in Vt. 152–53
  and Indian wars 18–26
French, William 48
Fresh air fund 174
Frost, Robert 201–202; *ill. 201*

Gaspée 60
Gazetteer 171
Geography (Vt.) 3–5
George III, King of England 32–
  33, 38, 45; *ill. 45*
Gettysburg, Battle of 138
Goesbriand, Bishop Louis de 152–
  53
Gore, John 179–80
Government (Vt.) 62–64, 78–79,
  89, 94–95, 102–105, 133–34,
  137–38, 174–75, 192–93
  See also Constitution (Vt.),
  Appendix III
Grange 166–67

Granite-quarrying 157–58
Grant, Charles Hampson 189
Grants, *see* New Hampshire
  Grants; Green Mountain
  Boys
Graye, Johne 12–14
Green Mountain(s)
  formation of 3–4
  hiking club 187
  Parkway 199–200, 205
Green Mountain Boys 95, 138
  in Canada 57–61
  in New York land dispute 36–
    41, 48–49, 87–88
  at Ticonderoga 50–56
Greylock, Chief 24–25
Griffith, D. W. 194
Guilford (Vt.) 49, 86–87

Haldimand Papers 83–85
Hale, Enoch 120
Halifax (Vt.) 179
Hall, Benjamin 105
Hall, Hiland 105
Hall, Samuel R. 119
Harris, Dr. Elisha 142–43
Harris, Fred 186
Hartness, James 190
Haswell, Anthony 91
Haynes, Lemuel 149–50
Hedge, Lemuel 125
Hemenway, Abby 171
Henderson, George Washington
  150–51
Highgate (Vt.) 202–203
Holy Rollers 112
Hoosick (N.Y.) 76–77
Hopkins, Samuel 98
Hospitals, *see* Medicine
Houghton, Daniel 48

House of Representatives (Vt.) 192–93, 200
Howard, Clarina (Mrs. Nichols) 114–16, 172
Howe, Jemima Sartwell 23
Hubbard, Ashabel 99
Hubbardton, Battle of 71

Ide, Annie 172–73
Ide, Deborah 166
Ide, Henry 172–73
Immigration (to Vt.) 89, 148–61
    See also Emigration; Population; Settlement; specific groups
Independence (Vt.) 66–68, 79–81
Independence, Declaration of (U.S.) 61–62
Independence, Fort 61–62, 70
Indian Captive, The 86
Indians (Vt.)
    major tribes 6–11
    raids against settlers 18–26, 85–86
    relations with France 11–12, 14–15, 18–26
Ingersoll, Jared 35–36
Inventions (Vt.) 98–100, 123–25, 189–90, 194–95
Irish (in Vt.) 153, 155
Iroquois Indians 8, 12, 18–19, 70
Italians (in Vt.) 157–58

Jackson, H. Nelson 180–81
Jarvis, William 127
Jennison, Silas 110
Jericho (Vt.) 183–85
Jews (in Vt.) 159
Jogues, Father Isaac 14–15
Johnson, Estelle S. 144

Johnson family (Indian captives) 22–23
Johnson, Willie 139
Jones, Reuben 46–47, 67
Judiciary (Vt.) 78, 89, 117
    See also Government
Jungle Book, The 174
Just So Stories, The 174

Kendall, Nicanor 99
Kilgore, Carrie Burnham 170
Kipling, Rudyard 174; ill. 174
Know-Nothing Party 154

"Lady Wentworth" 30
Lafayette, Marquis de 117, 120
Land-grant colleges 167–68
Land use 1–2, 72, 169, 205–206, 209–10
Lawrence, Jonathan 166–67
Legislation 1–2, 117, 133–34
    See also Constitution (Vt.); Judiciary (Vt.)
Legislature (Vt.), see Assembly; House of Representatives
Libraries (Vt.) 119, 158–59
Lincoln, President Abraham 136–37, 140
Lindbergh, Charles A. 190
Little, Henry 121–23
Long Pond 106–107
Long Trail 187
Lyndon (Vt.) 191
Lyon, Matthew 95–96

MacDonough, Thomas 106
Man and Nature 169
Manchester (Vt.) 31
Mansfield, Mount 3
Maple syrup 9

Marble-quarrying 158–59
Marsh, George Perkins 169–70
McKinley, William 174–75
Mead, Larkin 104
Medicine 42, 142–44
Memphremagog, Lake 5, 107
Merrill, Perry 198
Mexican War 133
Middlebury College 150
Millerites 113
Milne, William F. 187–88
Mining 156–59
Missionaries, Jesuit 14–15
    See also Religion
Mohican Indians 8
Money, issued in Vt. 91–92
Montgomery, General Richard
    59–60
Montpelier (Vt.) 103–105, 119,
    157–58, 160
Morey, Samuel 99
Morgan, Justin 126–27
Mormon Church 113–14
Morrill, Justin Smith 167–68; ill.
    167
Moving pictures 193–94
Munro, John 39

Nationalities (in Vt.) 148–61
    See also specific groups (Blacks,
    Irish, Scots, etc.)
New Connecticut 66–68
New Hampshire Grants 27–29,
    31 ff., 79–81
    See also Green Mountain Boys;
    Westminster "Massacre"
Newspapers 38, 41, 91
New York, land claims of (in Vt.)
    29, 31–41, 45–49, 63, 66–67,
    79–80, 86–88, 94

Nichols, Clarina Howard 114–16,
    172
Nineteenth Amendment 192
    See also Women's rights
Noyes, John Humphrey 113; ill.
    113
Number Four, Fort 22, 25
Nurses (Vt.)
    in American Revolution 77–78
    in Civil War 143–44
    in World War I 191

O'Callaghan, Father Jeremiah 112
Onion River Company 40
Organs, Estey 162–63
Orleans (Vt.) 150

Paleo Indians 7
Parks, State 198
Patents, see New York, land
    claims of
Patrons of Husbandry 166–67
Peacham (Vt.) 119
Peru (Vt.) 189
Phelps, Charles 86
Phelps, John W. 137
Phelps, Noah 51
Photography 184–85
Pioneering with Wild Flowers 204
Plymouth (Vt.) 165–66, 196
Poles (in Vt.) 159–60
Political parties (Vt.) 154
Politics, see Government
Population (Vt.) 31–32, 41, 89,
    94, 95, 132, 161, 205
    See also Appendix II; Emigra-
    tion; Immigration
Postal service (Vt.) 91
Potash, production of 92
Poultney (Vt.) 157, 159

Poverty, problems of, *see* Debtors
Pownal (Vt.) 31
Proctor (Vt.) 158–59
Proctor, Emily 158–59
Putney (Vt.) 113, 203
   Yorker uprising at 87

Radio 194–95
Railroads 129–30, 152–53, 181–83
Randolph (Vt.) 126–27
Recreation 164–66, 185–87, 198–
   99, 205
   See also Skiing; Youth activities
Redding, David 82–83
Redeemed Captive, The 20
Religion (Vt.) 14–15, 20–21, 97,
   110–14, 152–53, 159
Republic (Vt.), *see* Independence
   (Vt.)
Revolutionary War 49–88 *passim*
Roads (Vt.) 25, 120–21
   See also Transportation
Robinson, Beverly 83
Robinson, Molly 177–79
Robinson, Rowland 111, 134–35,
   177–79
Robinson, Samuel 29–30, 32
Rogers' Rangers 23–24
Rogers, Robert 23–24
"Rokeby" 177
Roosevelt, President Franklin 200,
   202–203
Runner, Dick 146–47
Rutland 138, 182, 189

St. Albans (Vt.) 155, 182
   raid on 141–42
St. Clair, Arthur 62, 70–71
St. Francis Indians 24–25
St. Frederic, Fort 16–17

St. Johns, Fort 55–56
St. Johnsbury 99–100, 172–73, 176,
   182, 190
St. Michael's College 161
Ste. Anne, Fort 16
Saratoga, Battle of 78
Schmitt, George 189
School for International Training
   161
Schools, *see* Education
Schuyler, General Philip 58–59,
   76
Scots (in Vt.) 149
Scott, Julian 139
Scott, William 139–40
Scouting 187–89
Settlement (of Vt.)
   18th century 16–23, 29–33, 41–
     44, 89
   19th century 148–61
   See also Population
Sheep 127
Sherwood, Justus 84
Skenesboro (Vt.) 70
Skiing 161, 186–87
Slate-mining (Vt.) 156–57
Slavery
   forbidden in Vt. 72
   issue of 114, 133–36
Smith, Elias 89–91
Smith, John G. 142
Smith, Joseph 114; *ill. 114*
Smuggler's Notch (Vt.) 105
Spaniards (in Vt.) 159–60
Spanish-American War 175–76
Springfield (Vt.) 99, 190
Stark, General John 76–77
Stark, Molly 77
Statehood (Vt.) 80–81, 94
State House 103–105, 157

Steamboats 99, 128–29
Steele, Zadock 85–86
Stevens, Henry 104–105
Stevenson, Robert Louis 172–73
Story, Ann 43–44
Stowe (Vt.) 160
Stratton Mountain 108–109
Suffrage, *see* Voting
Swedes (in Vt.) 156

Taconic Mountains 3
Taylor, James P. 187
Television 195
Thompson, Zadock 87–88, 101–103
Ticonderoga, Fort 25, 50–55, 70; *ill.* 50
Titus-Hazen, Fanny 144
Tomasi, Mari 157–58
Tories 74–79, 82–83
Transportation
    airplane 189–90
    automobile 179–81, 190
    railroad 129–30, 152–53, 181–83
    water 128–29
Trapp family 160–61
Treaty of Paris 26
Truman, President Harry 203
Twilight, Alexander 150
Tyler, Royall 105

Underground Railroad 134–35
United Nations 203
University of Vermont 117, 127, 150–51, 172
    Agricultural Extension Service 188
Unknown Heroine, An 147

Valcour, Battle of 64–66
Valentine, Alonzo 156
Van Metre, J. L. E. 145–47
Vermont
    origin of name 67–69
    University of 117
    See also Appendices
Vermont Gazette or Green Mountain Postboy, The 91
Vershire (Vt.) 156
Vikings (in Vt.) 13–14
Voting
    rights for men 72
    rights for women 114–16, 170, 172, 192–93

Wales, *see* Welsh
War(s)
    American Revolution 49–88 *passim*
    Civil 133–47
    1812 105–106
    French and Indian 18–26
    Mexican 133
    Spanish-American 175–76
    World War I 191–92
    World War II 200–201
Warner, Gideon 37
Warner, Seth 37, 57–61, 71, 77–78
Washington, George 58, 80–81
Water travel, *see* Transportation
Way Down East 194
Webster, Daniel 108–109
Welsh (in Vt.) 156–57
Wentworth, Benning 27–30; *ill.* 28
Westminster (Vt.)
    convention (1777) 66–67
    "Massacre" 44–49
Weston (Vt.) 156

White River Junction (Vt.) 193
Whitelaw, James 149
Wilder (Vt.) 188
Willard, Charles 190
Williams, Dr. Samuel 101
Williams, Rev. John 20
Wilmington (Vt.) 156
Wilson, James 98
Windmill Point (Vt.) 16
Windsor (Vt.) 99
    conventions at (1777) 69, 71–73
    first Assembly at 78–79
Windsor County (Vt.) 160
Women's rights 114–16, 170, 172,
    192–93
Wood, Lydia A. 144

Woodland Indians 8–11
Woodstock (Vt.) 89, 169, 186
World War I 191–92
World War II 200–201, 203

"Year of No Summer" 107–108
Yorkers, *see* New York; Boundary
    disputes
"Yorker War" 86–88
Young, Ammi B. 104
Young, Bennett 141–42
Young, Brigham 114; *ill. 114*
Young, Dr. Thomas 67–69
Youth activities 164–66, 177–79,
    185–89
    See also Children, role of